Chilling True Tales of Old Preston

Book 3

K. A. JOHNSON

First published November 1994 by
WINCKLEY PRESS,
5 Winckley Street,
Preston PR1 2AA

ISBN 0 907769-20-9

Set in 12 on 12 point Garamond
Designed and typeset by Winckley Press.
Printed and bound in Great Britain

The author, Keith Anthony
Johnson, is Preston born and
bred. He was initially educated
at St. Augustine's Roman
Catholic School, before
completing his studies at the
Harris College, Preston.
For many years he has had a
keen interest in local history and
in particular the lives of Preston
people of a bygone age.

He is a member of the
Lancashire Authors'
Association and the Crime
Writers' Association.

Married with two sons, he lives
and works in the town as an
engineering designer. Besides the
previous books in the 'Chilling
True Tales' series he is also the
author of the highly popular
book 'People of Old Preston'.

ACKNOWLEDGEMENTS

I am indebted to the journalists of a bygone era who described the events that took place in great detail. The reporters of the following newspapers deserve praise for their accounts of the past:

Preston Chronicle
Preston Guardian
Preston Herald
Lancashire Daily Post
Preston Pilot

I further acknowledge the assistance given to me by the staff of the Harris Reference Library in Preston – they are quite wonderful.

Patricia Crook
My thanks to Pat who put her literary skills, time and cheerful encouragement at my disposal. I will remain forever grateful.

Glen Crook
My thanks are extended to Glen for his enthusiastic commitment to the book's photographic requirement.

J C Fielding
Once again I wish to thank J C Fielding for providing line drawings and sketches.

BIBLIOGRAPHY

Whittle, P. *History of Preston* (1821).
Hardwick, C. *History of the Borough of Preston* (1857).
Hewitson, A. *History of Preston* (1883).
Griffiths, A. *Chronicles of Newgate* (1883).
Pilkington, W. *Then and Now* (1911).

INTRODUCTION

I WILL be delighted if you take this opportunity of accompanying me on a third trip into bygone Preston. No excuse is needed for embarking on a further journey into the annals of our town.

At this point it is perhaps appropriate to look at the nineteenth century through the eyes of a Prestonian of those distant days. Having been born amidst the poverty of the 1840's he was able, in the early years of the present century, to record a lifetime's recollections gathered during the reign of Queen Victoria.

In those seventy years, upwards of two thousand acres of land had been added to the township. The acres that once were covered with gardens and plantations, hills and hollows, winding lanes and smiling fields, had given way to industry, commerce, religion and education with their attendant buildings and structures.

Ancient landmarks had disappeared and historical mansions had been converted into places of business and colleges for learning. Old cotton mills had been turned into soap works, tea warehouses, furniture stores, flour mills, provision stores and places for preaching.

The 'cotton lords' had been the governors of Preston, with their residences in Winckley Square, but now they had retreated to their country seats. Gradually the town had moved into the hands of the lawyer, the doctor, the merchant and the shopkeeper, yet the cotton spinning and weaving was still the staple occupation of the townsfolk.

Soon after five o'clock each workday, the town resounded to the clang of the 'wooden shoon', as an army of thirty thousand pairs of wooden clogs hurried to all parts of the town. Somehow that industry had survived the years of the cotton famine when the great chimneys ceased to smoke and the spindles and looms became as hushed as if it was eternal night. It was a calamity indeed, which reduced honest and struggling poverty to a state of absolute humiliation and destitution. He had been there, and could well remember the great crowds – half fed, half clothed, miserable, dejected and sickly-looking.

Had it only been seventy years since the Marsh Lane area, on the outskirts of the town, had been regarded as a terror by all respectably dressed people? Rarely could a decent citizen walk through the area without being insulted, robbed or injured. The district had been occupied by a rougher element of humanity who were poor, reckless and ignorant. Caring neither for God, man nor devil. The people had grown up in heathenism, and the children had been trained for crime. The sacred hours of the Sabbath were spent in gambling, cockfighting, dog racing, pigeon flying and prizefighting. For a gallon of beer two men would have a hammer and tongs confrontation, punching with their clogs until their legs could not stand, and until their faces were bloodied and bruised.

The Police at that time were few, their number quite inadequate to keep the people under control. They had been treated with distrust, disgust and disrespect, but now at the dawn of a new century, they were regarded by most as the guardian angels of day and night. Keeping a watchful eye on the drunkard, the harlot, the thief, the forger, and the murderer and rendering a philanthropic service to their town, as they patrolled their beats.

Gone had the days of the public washing ground, such as the one at the top of Meadow Street. Whilst homes were not supplied with running water, the open-air washhouse had been the scene of great activity. Every day was a washing day, except Sunday. Many a mile they would carry their bundle to the washing ground. Placing their pans on a makeshift fireplace of bricks, they would obtain water from the surrounding pits. When the scrubbing and rubbing was done, if the weather was kind, they would dry their clothes upon the grass.

Progress had now been made. Houses were fitted with hot and cold water upstairs and down, and at many a home the laundry van called to collect the weekly wash.

No longer, at time of accident, was an injured person carried shoulder high on a shutter to the nearest public house – remaining there until fit to be removed home or else buried. The ambulance institution revolutionised that, and within a short time those in need of aid could be hurried to the Infirmary. A place where medicine had outstripped superstition, and where men were no longer bled, cupped, leeched or brandied. How had the human race survived an age when brandy, whisky and beer were the best the medical man could offer? Enormous had been the advances of medical science, in the lifetime of this one man.

His recollections led on to the founders of the Temperance Movement, who had preached teetotalism for all. He had known them all, he had walked and talked with them and listened to their rough eloquence in the old cockpit. They had seen the dens of infamy and crime, where moral wrecks were created by day and by night. Rushing to the rescue they had rung bells, made speeches, delivered lectures, given their money, sought subscriptions and established Societies. They had been hissed, misrepresented, boycotted, deserted, stoned and besieged.

Their very lives had been threatened and their buildings wrecked. But they ignored abuse and the tactics of opposition, to hammer home the principles of the new doctrine. Their movement was born in poverty, cradled in the storm, lived amid reproach and advanced into the teeth of the opposition. In all, they revolutionised the administration of the licensing laws, inspired the police with zeal and activity, changing the habits and customs of society. As a body they had driven back despair, and opened a new door of hope leading the way to social reform.

The man who left this legacy of information was Mr. W. Pilkington in his publication 'Then and Now'. He completed it by recording the Prestonian's right to be proud. He believed it was no vain thing to have been born in Preston, and saw no harm in exhibiting a manly satisfaction in his good fortune. We could be proud of our industries populated with work people who were earnest and full of grit. In his town there was now more intellectual zeal and religious fervour than ever in the past. Learning had become no longer the privilege of the few but the heritage of the many.

His Preston, had the best of market places, the Gothic-style Town Hall, the handsome Miller Arcade, the noble Sessions Hall, the magnificent Harris Free Library and Museum, the modernised Public Hall and the impressive headquarters of the Lancashire County Council in Fishergate. This Proud Preston could not boast a castle, abbey or cathedral, but it was a town of churches, Sunday schools and missions. In this respect, relative to population, it did not rank second to any town in the Kingdom. For all to see were many imposing edifices that added greatly to the town's architectural attractiveness. In recognition of the work done by those who spread the secular word, he remarked:

"If all the men and women who are in touch with Christian work were taken out of Preston, and all the churches and Sunday Schools were closed only for one year, what a hell this town would become!"

To hell and back our ancestors may have been, so it's not surprising that yet more tales unfold. Back through the reign of Queen Victoria and beyond, the people of our town endured all that human souls could bear. Of course there was good and evil, honesty and deceit, happiness and sadness, riches and poverty. Indeed, all the opposites that lead to the trials and tribulations of everyday life. Let's therefore glimpse again the world of our forefathers, and while we do so, be neither Judge nor Jurymen, but spare some compassion for their situation.

Keith A. Johnson

CONTENTS

SWEETHEART SLAIN BY JILTED LOVER

TOWARDS the end of July, 1868 the 'Preston Chronicle' news-paper carried the headline – 'Shocking Murder of a Sweetheart' – going on to inform the readers of a terrible tragedy that had recently taken place on the outskirts of Preston. The determined murder had taken place near Drumhead – a sequestered spot between Walton-le-Dale and Preston. The tragedy involved nineteen-years-old Elizabeth Brindle and Charles Hamer, aged twenty. The pair were employed at Mr. Bourne's Mill, Brindle, where Charles Hamer's father was the manager over the weaving department. Miss Brindle worked as a weaver, and the manager's son as a clothlooker.

For about three years Miss Brindle had been on intimate terms with Charles Hamer and for over twelve months their intimacy had developed into an attachment, the pair being looked upon as lovers. Hamer regarded the young woman as his future partner and often visited Higher Shuttlingfields Farm, the home of her parents, to pay court to her.

He was undoubtedly particularly fond of her and he had a jealous nature if she did not receive his addresses in the proper spirit. He was punctual and regular in his visits and the couple were often seen walking out together.

Hamer had what could best be described as a delicate frame and over a period of time he gradually gave himself up to the use of tobacco in excess. This habit was obnoxious to the girl and on more than one occasion she chastised him for his indulgence in smoking and chewing tobacco, telling him he was impairing his health by it.

Towards the end of June, 1868, Miss Brindle had again reason to find fault with his habits and told him if he would be less indulgent it may be the means of making him stronger. Pointing out that if he did not cease using tobacco, she would most certainly refuse to receive his addresses in the future.

Hamer took offence at this decision on the part of his young lady, and both parties thinking themselves wronged, decided not to speak to the other. Despite their differences, Hamer continued to

1

visit the home of Miss Brindle and on a Sunday night in the middle of July he paid a visit which lasted over an hour. During the visit no words passed between the young couple who were in the company of the girl's parents.

The following Wednesday morning Miss Brindle, on her arrival at the mill, received a letter signed by Hamer asking her to meet him that evening in Martin's Field, through which she would have to travel on her way from the mill to her home.

For several days there had been a marked change in Hamer's conduct. He seemed to be sorely distressed about something and he continually refused to take his meals.

On that Wednesday evening, shortly before the hands at the mill ceased work, he went to the blacksmith's workshop and ground an old dessert knife, which was about the length of an ordinary pocket knife. He was observed doing this, but no suspicions were formed as to what he intended doing with it.

On leaving the mill, Miss Brindle, who was one of a family of eight children, was accompanied by one of her sisters, who likewise was employed at the mill as a weaver. On their way she mentioned the receipt of the letter and said if Hamer met her she would not be afraid of him. Telling her sister that she would inform him at once that she would have nothing more to do with him, as she was determined not to be trodden upon by him any longer.

As they approached Martin's Field the sisters observed Hamer about 100 yards in the distance. Elizabeth Brindle then told her sister she would wait for him to reach her and her sister carried on towards home.

A few minutes later Hamer was met in Alma Row going in the direction of Gregson Lane, by a person of his acquaintance called James Yates. Hamer's hands were covered with blood and there was blood upon his cheeks. His features had an unsettled aspect and hanging down from under his jacket was a rope. Yates asked him what was the matter, but Hamer made no reply and hurried on his way.

Continuing his journey James Yates next entered Martin's Field and there he found Miss Brindle stretched upon the ground. Her throat and neck were cut in three places and from two of the wounds blood flowed copiously. About two yards away were her basket, shawl and bonnet. Her dress and person were so much covered with blood that it was only by examination of the bonnet and basket that he realised who it was.

He spoke to her twice before he could obtain an answer, and then she spoke his name and took hold of his hand. She then said, "Charles Hamer has stuck me, because I would not go with him. He has gone a doing himself. I wish I was out of my punishment."

James Yates at once raised the alarm, a doctor from Preston was sent for and the police officer at Higher Walton was informed. The unfortunate girl was conveyed home as quickly as possible, where her distraught parents and the many helpers did everything they could to preserve her life.

A messenger had travelled to the home of Preston surgeon William Henry Spencer, in Church Street, but by the time he had driven his conveyance to the home of the girl, she had expired. His examination of the body revealed that the carotid artery and jugular vein had been completely severed. The wounds showed that her assassin had not only been desperate in his efforts, but had a very accurate knowledge of the most vulnerable and fatal points of attack.

While the efforts had been taking place to save the life of his victim, Hamer was hurrying from the dreadful scene and heading towards Mintholme Wood. Before he reached his destination he came across his brother William, who caught hold of him by the jacket and observed that his hands were covered in blood. He asked him had he been killing someone and he replied that he had been fighting at Moon's Mill and that a policeman was after him. Hamer then gave his brother a slip of paper, with a request that he hand it to their father and, releasing himself from his brother's grip, he ran away.

The killing of Elizabeth Brindle had taken place about seven o'clock and two hours later a weaver named James Preston made a startling discovery. Walking through Mintholme Wood he saw the body of Charles Hamer suspended from a tree, the rope around his neck was in about four folds. Assistance was soon on hand and when cut down the body was still warm.

The report of the tragedy spread with great rapidity from mouth to mouth and the greatest of excitement prevailed. Crowds of people rushed to the spot where Miss Brindle had been slain, and it was obvious from the ground where she was found, that a severe struggle had taken place between the poor girl and her antagonist. From the blood upon the ground it appeared that the girl had, after being attacked, walked through a stile and some 70 yards beyond it before she had fallen through sheer exhaustion.

The tragedy cast a sad gloom over the district and before the week was out the evening's events were relived at the Inquests on the bodies. These were held at the Black Horse public house in Higher Walton and the Preston Coroner, Miles Myers, Esquire, was in attendance.

The letter that Charles Hamer had sent to his father was read out by the Coroner. In it Hamer ordered his watch, books etc. to be given to his relatives and he asked for his body to be interred along with that of his victim. If that could not be done he requested that he be buried beside his grandmother at Blackburn. One of those called said he had seen Hamer writing the note

Miles Myres, the Preston Coroner, concluded that 'wilful murder' had taken place

on the forenoon of the fatal day and that on completion Hamer had folded it and placed it in his pocket.

Relatives and work colleagues alike testified as to the strange behaviour of Hamer during the days prior to the dreadful incident. His mother told how he had not eaten properly for days and that there had been no smile upon his face since he had fallen out with his sweetheart.

It was apparent from the witnesses called that there had been some differences between them as is general with courting couples. There was not, though, any reason to suspect an outcome of such tragic proportions.

When the Coroner addressed the inquest jury relative to the death of Elizabeth Brindle, he told them their verdict must be one of "Wilful Murder." Without a moment's hesitation the jury expressed their fullest agreement and announced, "Wilful Murder by Charles Hamer."

The evidence in respect of the suicide of Hamer was then reviewed and Mr. Myers told the jury that it was necessary for them to consider the state of mind of Hamer, when he committed the murder and destroyed his own life.

The writing of the note to the father clearly showed that he had undoubtedly contemplated the murder before he committed it and also planned his own death afterwards. A consideration for the jury was whether by neglecting his food and working himself into a desperate state he had brought himself to a position where he did not understand what he was doing.

After a deliberation of about half an hour the jury decided that Hamer was of sound mind at the time of the tragedy and as a result they returned a verdict of *felo de se.*

The request of Charles Hamer to be buried alongside his sweetheart was denied. A couple of nights after the inquest, shortly before midnight, he was interred in Brindle churchyard, in an unconsecrated portion of the graveyard without religious ceremony.

SHOCKING TRAGEDY NEAR PRESTON.

A YOUNG WOMAN MURDERED BY A DISCARDED SWEETHEART.

On Wednesday night a shocking and determined murder was committed at a place near Drumhead,—a sequestered spot between Walton-le-Dale and Preston—resulting in the death of a young woman named Elizabeth Brindle.

The deceased was about 18 years of age, and lived with her parents, at a place called Shuttling-fields Farm. She was employed at Bourne's cotton mill, in Brindle; and at this factory there worked a young man named Hamer.

About twelve months ago an intimacy sprang up between Hamer and the deceased, and for some time they "kept company" in a very quiet and, apparently, agreeable manner. Recently a coolness was observed between them, and this eventuated in direct indifference on the part of the deceased. It has not transpired from what the indifference arose; but that a "difficulty" did exist between them is certain; and that the deceased was the more aggrieved party (in her own estimation) is also be-

The Preston Guardian informed its readers of the tragedy.

FIRE RAGING IN PRESTON MARKET PLACE

S HORTLY before one o'clock on the morning of Wednesday, 21st March, 1860, two of the staff of the 'Preston Guardian' newspaper, after completing a late night shift, headed home through Preston town centre. On reaching the top of Cannon Street, they heard a lot of noise emanating from the Market Place.

Curious as to the cause of the disturbance, they hurried to the Market Place whereupon they saw the premises of Mr. T. B. Dick, grocer and tea dealer, in flames. The establishment formed part of a high pile of buildings on the north side of the square, being in fact four storeys high. The second storey resembled a furnace, and the flames were ascending with fearful rapidity.

At the windows of the third storey stood some human beings, who were not distinctly discernible in consequence of the dense smoke. They were frantically shouting for aid, and hesitating between destruction from within or the perils of a leap into the street, a descent of from eight to ten yards, with the prospect before them of death or a lasting injury.

In the street below, screaming and running wildly about were some half dozen spectators, among whom were two or three women, whose agonizing shrieks in conjunction with the appeals of the ill-fated inmates above, lent a horror to the scene which could not easily be erased from the memory.

One of the 'Preston Guardian' reporters hastened to the fire station, only to discover that the alarm had already been given. Mr. Marriott the superintendent of the brigade and four or five of his men, had fastened the ropes to one engine, the bell summoned the remainder to their post, and in an instant they were on their way down Lord Street and through New Street, to the scene of the disaster.

Within minutes, the water pipes were attached to plugs in the front of the engine, and an immense volume of water was pitched upon the flames which speedily began to quell.

In the middle of a March night in 1860, Preston market place was a scene of terror as flames engulfed the premises of Mr. T. B. Dick.

Prior to the arrival of the fire brigade, three of the inmates had made the awful leap for life. The heat and smoke being perfectly unendurable, they had no other resource left, and Mr. Dick, with an infant in his arms, dropped into the street amid the exclamations of the terror-stricken beholders. In his descent he came in contact with a projection over the shop window and, as a consequence, lost hold of the six month old child, the pair of them falling asunder.

Mr. Dick was taken up and at once conveyed into the White Horse public house, where the landlord rendered all the assistance he could. The infant, like a little waif, was picked up by some person, who ran about with it for a while before ultimately handing it to the care of Mrs. Benjamin from the tailor's shop opposite.

The third person who took the desperate leap was a young woman, a servant, who fell a considerable way into the Market Place, and was carried immediately into one of the shops opposite, where she was stretched out at full length, in an apparently insensible condition.

At this time there were very few people about, and all was confusion and dismay. A messenger was despatched to the nearest surgeon, Mr. Richardson, in Cannon Street, and he was speedily on the spot, followed by other leading medical men, including Dr. Spencer, Mr. Halden and Mr. Pilkington, who rendered all the aid it was in their skill to devise.

Mr. Dick kept inquiring as to the infant who had shared his fate, and it was removed to the White Horse and afterwards to the George Inn, where it was tenderly nursed by the landlady. The servant who had received a severe bruise upon the forehead, but was pronounced as not to be dangerously injured, was conveyed to the White Horse where she received the requisite attendance.

The inquiries as to the fate of Mrs. Dick were numerous and touching, and it was at first supposed that she was still within the burning building. Great, however, was the joy when it was found that she had effected her escape by the back part of the premises. She was scorched upon the face and her hands were burnt in a pitiful manner; but outbuildings broke her fall and she was received by some parties who were trying to make an opening at the back of the premises. Being in her nightdress, she was wrapped in blankets and also conveyed to the White Horse.

The firemen continued to work the hose with all their might and main. They mounted ladders, back and front, and from four pipes discharged a great volume of water through the windows into the various rooms and over the top of the edifice, in order to stem the progress of the flames upwards. They were anxious to save life, for the terrible truth became known that in the front room of the uppermost storey, were sleeping another female servant, Elizabeth Billington, and the elder child of Mr. and Mrs. Dick, a four-year-old boy called Quentin.

T. B. Dick, grocer and tea dealer, was a popular proprietor – an advertisement in verse attracted customers.

8

The knowledge of this fact filled the spectators with horror and inspired the brigade to even greater efforts. All the while Mr. and Mrs. Dick frantically inquired after the fate of the child and his ill-fated partner in the chamber of death. The firemen worked incessantly and eventually Mr. Marriott and some of his men entered the premises. They made their way up the stairs, playing the hoses upon the flames, and making every effort in their mortal power to reach the room where the two were sleeping.

By ten minutes before two o'clock the flames were subdued sufficiently to enable the firemen to enter the room of the sleepers. The fire had not touched that part of the building, but the ascending smoke and heat had done their work. There was to be no waking; the little boy lay dead in his crib in one corner, suffocated; and in the other corner of the room was the corpse of the unfortunate woman, her flesh scorched. She had to all appearances risen from her bed and tried to get to the window, but had been struck down before she reached it.

The bodies were wrapped in sheets and carried to the White Horse where the sufferers, who had escaped their terrible end, were receiving the attention of the medical men.

A large quantity of wood had been used in the construction of the building and as a consequence it had burnt with fearful rapidity. The fire was believed to have started in the sitting room immediately over the shop and the property damage was mainly confined to the second and third storeys.

From an early hour of the morning there were vast crowds of spectators around the premises, which both internally and externally, appeared a disastrous wreck. Those gathered expressed great sympathy for the sufferers of the calamity, the greatest interest being shown for their fate and condition.

The morning bulletin stated that Mr. Dick still lay in a precarious state, that Mrs. Dick appeared to be much disfigured, and that the servant woman was more seriously injured than was first thought.

The fire brigade were praised for their excellent efforts, the main regret was that the brigade was not provided with fire escapes as used by other brigades in large towns. It was felt that, had they possessed apparatus of that kind, they may have been able to prevent the loss of human life.

On the Saturday morning the body of 14-year-old Elizabeth Billington was interred at Goosnargh and on the following Monday a funeral procession made its way to Preston Cemetery, where the boy Quentin Dick was laid to rest.

That afternoon at the Police-court, the final Inquest took place into their deaths. Fire officers and policemen gave evidence and re-called the horrors of the night. Inspector Marriott of the fire-brigade told the gathering that he had examined the premises, including the sitting room where the fire originated. He had found a defect in the flue behind the fire grate, in the brickwork, where the wooden joists ran close by. Part of the joists had burnt away and in his opinion sparks from the fire in that grate had been the likely cause of the blaze.

In all the inquiry lasted for over three hours and, going over the evidence, the Coroner stated that he was satisfied that the deaths had been caused purely by accident and that no person was to blame. He asked the jury to consider not only their verdict but also to con-sider making recommendations that may help to avoid such a catas-trophe in the future.

After conferring together for a few minutes the jury returned a verdict of 'Accidental Death by burning or suffocation'. They ac-companied their verdict with the following recommendations for the relative authorities:
   that the fire brigade should be equipped with fire escapes;
   that the fire brigade should be furnished with lamps, so as not
   to rely on the police providing them as on this occasion;
   and that a new and more powerful alarm bell be substituted for
   the present one at the fire engine station.

The Coroner thanked the jury for their deliberations and as-sured them that their suggestions would be forwarded to the proper quarters.

Postscript:

The fire brigade station in Tithebarn Street was erected in 1852 and before that time the brigade had their quarters at the old Lock-Up in Avenham Street. Mr. Henry Marriott was the first brigade superin-tendent, being appointed in 1854. Prior to that time the duties of brigade superintendent were carried out by the Chief Constable of the Borough. Mr. Marriott remained in his post until his death in January, 1884 at which time he was interred, with brigade honours, in the Preston Cemetery.

RUFFIANS AND ROGUES
ARMED WITH PISTOLS

IN 1835 the Municipal Corporation Act was passed and as a result 170 Boroughs were required to organise completely independent police forces, controlled by the local Watch Committee. Preston was by this time one of the more fortunate Boroughs, having already an effective police force. This had been established under a Corporation Act some 20 years earlier, when Thomas Walton was made Preston's first Chief Constable.

Of course, the surrounding areas were not quite so fortunate and this was highlighted by events in the autumn of 1824, which led to a trial, at Lancaster Assizes, the following March.

For a considerable amount of time Leyland and its neighbourhood had been the scene of almost nightly depredation from a gang of ruffians. So frequent and alarming became the outrages of the gang that it was not merely deemed unsafe to be on the highway after nightfall, but it was found necessary to employ watchmen to protect the property of the inhabitants during the dark winter nights.

The situation came to a head on the night of the 25th of October, 1824 when a gang of diabolical wretches broke into the dwelling house of a Mrs. Anders in Clayton-le-Woods. That night Mrs. Anders was awoken by the barking of her dog and on getting up she went to the window, which she was in the act of opening when a pistol was fired at her.

Seeing four men rushing across the yard with obvious intent to enter the premises, she began to scream, an act which woke her sister and the servant man, Bartholomew Cutler. The man immediately rose, shut the sisters in their room and made his escape from the house, which the villains had by now entered, with a view to obtaining assistance from neighbours.

Before he could reach the gate a pistol was fired at him and the whole of the gang joined in the pursuit. The servant man was soon caught and overpowered and given a vicious beating by the four men. One of them struck him with an iron crowbar and the others kicked and punched him in a most savage manner. Only on a promise that he would return to the house and show them where the valuables were hidden, did they spare his life.

They then commenced the work of plunder, but their endeavours were interrupted when they heard a horse galloping around outside. Fearing that assistance had arrived the gang abandoned their evil activities and fled from the premises. In fact, the animal that had frightened the robbers away was only a colt from a neighbouring field, which had been disturbed by the noise of the pistol.

The thieves had disguised themselves by blacking their faces and wearing their coats wrong side out. Cutler though had, in the past, made the acquaintance of Robert Robinson, who played the leading role in the robbery and, despite his disguise, recognised him from his speech. When Cutler had asked the men what they wanted Robinson had replied, "We'll let thee know what we want," in his unmistakable tones.

An immediate search was at once undertaken for the perpetrators of the crime and three men were soon apprehended, they being the Robinson brothers Henry aged 25, Robert aged 34 and Thomas Rigby, aged 22.

A number of people had seen them in the neighbourhood that night, including William Ollerton who on returning from Preston, shortly before midnight, had met the three along with another, on the highway. He had been puzzled by their behaviour as they passed him, because they had seemed anxious to avoid him by hiding their faces.

Upon their arrest there had been traces of soot blacking on their foreheads and in their hair, and some of the discarded plunder had been recovered not far from where they lived.

There was uncertainty, however, about the identity of the gang's fourth member and as a result only the three of them stood upon their trial at Lancaster Assizes. The trial caused quite a lot of interest when it took place on the second Friday in March, 1825. The desperate gang of burglars had the evidence stacked against them and the manner in which the man servant had been treated led to the full weight of the law being applied to them.

Once a 'Guilty' verdict had been delivered, His Lordship, Mr. Justice Bayley reminded the three of them of the way they had used their pistols to put innocent lives at risk. He then implored them all to prepare for the worst, and solemnly pronounced sentence of death.

12

The use of pistols was becoming an all too common reality and during that same Assizes Robert Latus a 17-year-old cotton spinner from Preston, stood before Mr. Justice Bayley, accused of wilful and malicious shooting at the person of Thomas Hesketh, who, like himself, was employed at Mr. Caton's cotton factory in Back Lane, which stood close to Trinity Church. Latus had resented the fact that Hesketh had gained employment at the same factory, due to a long-standing dislike they had harboured for each other.

Subsequently, a couple of days after Christmas in 1824, while Thomas Hesketh was on his way to work at six o'clock in the morning in the company of Mary Naylor, he was met by Robert Latus and another. Words were exchanged and then in the gloom of a winter's morning, Robert Latus produced a pistol, fired at Thomas Hesketh and then fled from the scene. Some of the shot hit Hesketh on the breast and some entered his clothing. Fortunately, the shot did little damage and within a fortnight he had fully recovered.

In the darkness of the morning there had been some doubt as to the identity of the attacker, but Mary Naylor was positive that Robert Latus was responsible. In fact, as he ran away, she had shouted after him, "I know thee, thou knows I know thee."

On Thursday the 30th of December, 1824 Mr. Walton, the Chief Constable of Preston was confident enough to take Robert Latus into custody. Especially after a man had come forward to state that he had exchanged the pistol for a watch at Latus's request and when another recalled selling him a quantity of detonating balls for the same pistol.

On a number of occasions, Latus was quizzed as to who was accompanying him that morning, but his only reply was, "I know you want me to tell you who the other was, but I never shall."

The case occupied little time in the Crown Court and despite a couple of witnesses testifying as to the good character of the prisoner, the Jury had little hesitation in finding him 'Guilty'. Mr. Justice Bayley then informed him that he was sentenced to death.

Later that day William Gillow, aged 25, was indicted for maliciously shooting, with intent to kill, Denis Carter, a gamekeeper to Mr. Hoghton. The prisoner and three other poachers had been detected in a game reserve at Walton-le-Dale. In an attempt to avoid capture, the prisoner had fired two shots at the gamekeeper. Once again His Lordship, having received a 'Guilty' verdict from the Jury, pronounced sentence of death.

Before the Assizes were completed, it was announced that the sentence of death recorded against Henry Robinson and Thomas Rigby, the Clayton-le-Woods burglars, Robert Latus from Preston and William Gillow of Walton-le-Dale, had been replaced by imprisonment until such time as His Majesty's Pleasure be known.

As a result the only person left for execution was the 34-year-old Robert Robinson. During his final days he showed no disposition to profit from religious counsel, although he did acknowledge that the baneful practice of drinking, swearing and Sabbath breaking, had led to his wretched situation.

His final day on earth was Saturday, April 2nd, 1825 and as the midday hour approached the most breathless anxiety prevailed. Once upon the scaffold he gazed about with apparent unconcern, until recognising in the crowd many of his companions, to whom he nodded and called out, "Fellows, take care of false witnesses."

However, when the hangman, Edward Barlow, adjusted the rope around his neck, his previous hardihood appeared to fail him and it was only with some difficulty that he could be held up – to be launched into eternity.

His body, after hanging the usual time was, at the request of a friend, given to them and conveyed to Leyland, where it was 'laid in state' at the house of his mother for the inspection of the curious.

The old woman herself, acting the part of chief mourner, pointing out the marks on the neck to the numerous visitors. To receive the 'favours' of such as went to see the corpse, two basins were placed near the body and upwards of ten pounds was collected by this inhuman exhibition.

He was buried the following Monday, when an immense crowd, numbering over two thousand, attended. While providing a Christian burial the Rev. Gardener Baldwin took the opportunity of illustrating the fate that awaited an evil course of life.

Hangman Edward 'Ned' Barlow despatched the victim from this life

POISONING OF MARY COOKSON

ON Sunday 22nd of January, 1837 at half past two o'clock in the afternoon William Cookson, who carried on the trade of a butcher, called at the Friargate shop of druggist, Mr. Beaumont. In accordance with the law concerning the supply of drugs, he had with him a man called James Dewhurst, who verified his identity when he requested an ounce of arsenic. Cookson telling the proprietor that he required the mixture for an itch disorder. The druggist charged him fourpence for the arsenic and warned him that it was a deadly poison. The purchaser replying that he would observe caution and take care to mix a sufficiently large quantity of water with it.

Later that afternoon, Cookson, who had been separated from his wife for about a month, turned up at the home of Catherine Whewell, an acquaintance of some six years. It was common knowledge that Cookson had been asked to quit the family home in Sudell's Yard, due to his violent conduct towards his wife, and he was in low despondent mood as he poured his troubles out to Catherine Whewell.

He told her that he didn't know what would be the end of all the troubles, but thought it would be something serious. Going on to say that, whether he or his wife died first, he hoped their friends would bury them at Longridge. Despite the woman's attempts to raise his spirits, he left her home in the same desolate state that he had arrived.

At about seven o'clock that evening, Cookson was seen by a neighbour trying to open the front door of his former home. The neighbour had seen Mary Cookson, her lodger John Brown, and a couple of the Cookson's children leave the house a few minutes earlier. Finding the front door fast, the estranged husband went down the side passage to the back door, and out of view of the watching neighbour who hoped he was on a mission of reconciliation.

The next sighting of Cookson that evening was in a nearby spirit vault where he asked for two-pennyworth of rum. With his rum he wanted sympathy but he remained in a desolate spirit and, when the barmaid offered to drink to good health, he replied that it was too late for good wishes to benefit him.

The following morning Mary Cookson got up a little before eight o'clock and immediately set about making herself a pot of tea. She took the teapot from its place on the staircase window, and as was her usual custom, for economic reasons, added some fresh tea to the leaves already in the pot.

Pouring herself a teacup full of tea she began to drink it, and immediately found its effects to make her throat sore, and her breast smart, and she began to feel very unwell. She then went upstairs and vomited, and suspecting that it must have been the tea that had produced the painful symptoms, she returned to the kitchen and examined the teapot. The leaves seemed to have a white appearance, so she took them out of the pot, and put them upon a plate.

Highly suspicious of the contents of the teapot, Mrs. Cookson at once took them across the street to Mr. Gilbertson, a local druggist. Upon her request the druggist began to test the mixture and upon smelling it he at once supposed that arsenic had been mixed with the tea. He then tested the contents by ammonia and nitrate of silver, by

Preston's old Town Hall, demolished in 1862. In January 1837, William Cookson stood in the large room used for police court purposes, accused of poisoning his wife.

sublimation, and in other ways that indicated his suspicions were correct. He detected the presence of as much as three grains of arsenic, a quantity sufficient to destroy many human lives.

At this time Mrs. Cookson was still feeling the effects of the poison and was at once taken home to bed, under the care of Mr. Spencer the surgeon. Fortunately the almost instant sickness and vomiting had kept the poison out of her system, and with the surgeon's guidance she began to recover.

The authorities were informed at once of the suspicious situation and an officer was sent to apprehend her husband. He appeared agitated when informed of Mrs. Cookson's ordeal and on his way into custody he attempted to let fall a small white paper packet which on examination contained a kind of paste. This being according to the husband, the ointment for his bad leg, and when analysed it was found to be a mix of meal and arsenic.

The following morning William Cookson appeared before the Magistrates at the Town Hall, charged with attempting to poison his wife of twelve years. The accused was quite well known in the town having been some six years previous the landlord of the Legs of Man Inn, in Fishergate.

Mrs. Cookson attended the hearing, but appeared to be suffering from the effects of the plot against her life, and from feelings of sickness was obliged to leave the crowded hall to get fresh air immediately after she had finished her depositions.

Two witnesses testified as to seeing the accused enter Mrs. Cookson's home on the Sunday evening, while she was out and it was shown without doubt that William Cookson had purchased the poison.

Not surprisingly the proceedings terminated with the accused being committed to Lancaster Castle to await trial.

The trial took place at the Lancaster Lent Assizes towards the end of March 1837 and William Cookson was accused of attempting to administer poison to his wife, with intent to murder her. With great firmness he pleaded 'not guilty' but the evidence was stacked against him and despite a speech of great power and eloquence from the defence representative, there was little hope for him. The Judge told the Jury to reach their verdict on the evidence and not to be swayed by considering the consequences for the prisoner.

The Jury gave the matter serious deliberation and after a considerable time returned into the court with a 'Guilty' verdict.

At once the prosecution, speaking on behalf of the wife, begged that his Lordship extend the mercy of the court so far as to spare the prisoner's life. To which request the Judge did not respond but merely ordered the prisoner to be removed, and brought back next day for sentencing.

The next morning, His Lordship began by seriously admonishing William Cookson for the heinousness of the crime of which he had been convicted. He then brought the case to an end by informing the prisoner that he would be transported for the term of his natural life.

When Cookson got back to the cells he learnt that he would be accompanied in his journey 'across the seas' by another Preston man. That man being Michael Riley, who had been found 'Guilty' at the same Assizes of the manslaughter of George Dessantes after a fight in Friargate in November 1836. Riley being arrested after a drunken brawl near to the Boars Head public house, during which he had stabbed his victim three times in the belly. His sentence was one of transportation for fourteen years.

The two men would be despatched from Lancaster en route to Australia's Botany Bay, on the first transport ship available. The convict ships were an unhealthy mode of transport and those that survived the journey of twelve thousand miles, faced a hard and brutal existence. Chained and shackled, the convicts were at the mercy of the officers, who could be cruel and vindictive.

A verse written in 1842 at a time when many convicted criminals were transported for their offences

Farewell Address

The assizes they are over now, the judge is gone away,
But many aching hearts are left within the town today;
Tho' crime is bad, yet poverty's made many one to be
A transport from his native land, and cross the raging sea.

Oh! 'Tis a cruel sentence for a man to leave his wife,
His children, and his dearest friends, all dearer than his life;
To leave the land that gave him birth, to see it p'rhaps no more,
And drag a wretched life in chains, upon\a distant shore.

Their sentence some deserve to get, and laws were made to be
Preservers of the public peace, and of society;
But great distress and want of work, starvation and disease,
Make inmates for a prison house, and transports for the seas.

Oh would our rulers make a law for man to earn his bread,
And make sufficient wage to keep his wife and children fed,
The judges would have less to do, and half their pay might be
Devoted to this public good, and bless society.

The prisons would be empty soon, and transport ships would then
Bring o'er the seas a load of corn, and not a load of men;
Act after Act our rulers make, but one they will not do,
To do unto others as they would — themselves be done unto.

Would they but pass an Act for man to work and earn his bread,
Crime would soon dwindle from the land, and transportation fled;
Would providence direct their hearts to make such laws, and then
Instead of outlawed slaves — we might have free and honest men.

Transportation Across the Seas

PRIOR to 1783 the convicts from these shores had been shipped out to the American colonies. Their sentence being worked out under a master who employed them. Then the United States of America announced that they did not want any more of those 'unruly immigrants'.

For the next couple of years those awaiting transportation were kept in disused rotting ships on the River Thames. Eventually a suggestion was made that Australia, some twelve thousand miles away, would be an excellent place in which to harbour them. Captain Cook had sailed round the coast and discovered a place he called Botany Bay, on account of its wonderful flowers and vegetation. With that place chosen for a convict settlement, Captain Arthur Phillips thus embarked with the first ship load of felons.

When the vessel arrived at that place Captain Phillips decided it was not suitable for the purpose and went further on, eventually landing at Port Jackson (now called Sidney Harbour). Despite the change of settlement the colony retained the name of Botany Bay.

In all Captain Phillips laboured hard for four years to establish the colony before he retired due to ill health. Those in his charge were a mixed band ranging from desperate criminals to men who had simply stolen food. England's criminal laws were harsh to the extreme and in consequence all manner of people were transported. In fact, in 1816 a law was passed punishing with seven years transportation any person found in possession of a net for taking rabbits. The Statute-Book allowing for over two hundred offences, mostly forms of stealing, to be punished by death. In reality the juries refused to convict for such offences as stealing apples, so that many of the so-called 'crimes' received no punishment.

As a result of the penal system no less than seventy-five thousand persons were transported to Botany Bay between 1787 and 1836, some for serious crimes, but many for offences such as sheep stealing.

The government had shown little imagination in the initial setting up of the settlement and from the start Captain Phillips had been short of supplies. He needed food, seeds and farm implements as more and more convicts poured into his colony. In consequence the food ran short and had to be strictly rationed. Often the soldiers entrusted with guarding the convicts and the rations were as thievish and dishonest as those in their care. Some of the convicts escaped into the bush and became 'bush rangers'. They became a terror to everyone, living a desperate existence. Those that were recaptured were sent to the dreaded Norfolk Island colony in the Pacific, a place of horrors kept for the worst offenders.

Within a few years a change came to the colony with the introduction of sheep, an officer taking eight Merino sheep into the settlement. They prospered on the grassy lands and this led to a rush of fortune-hunters from England who developed 'sheep stations' and employed convict labour to tend them.

Soon the free settlers were to outnumber the convicts and within a hundred years the number of sheep in the country was to total over 100 million.

Many of the convicts, sentence complete, were to later become prosperous and their children were to grow tall and healthy. Having a better chance than if they had been born in an English slum.

After a time the free settlers wished Australia to become respectable and they objected to the system of transportation. In consequence the last convicts were shipped to Australia in 1852.

TRAGEDY AT THE 'BIG FACTORY'

IN Guild Year, 1822 there was in the Salmon Street, Fishwick, area of the town an extensive cotton mill erected, which belonged to Messrs. Swainson, Birley and Company. The mill was known at the time as the 'Big Factory' as it was said to be seven storeys high, 158 yards long and 18 yards broad, containing 660 windows and no less than 32,000 panes of glass.

This mill was regarded as one of the wonders of its day and the tragic incident that took place there, on Thursday, November 22nd, 1849, made it the talk of the town. What occurred was one of those incidents, so simple in their origin yet so shocking and fatal in their effect, which frequently took place where machinery was worked by steam power.

On the morning in question, shortly after six o'clock, Thomas Lawson, a labourer, employed in the mill yard, was at work endeavouring to locate the source of a leakage in the main gas pipe. He had an open oil lamp with him to give sufficient light to enable him to work on a dark winter's morning. He placed the lamp down on the ground near to a small sewer and close to a detached building, which was used as a weaving shed. The sewer ran in the direction of the gas pipe and it appears that unbeknown to him, the sewer must have been filled with gas from the leakage he was seeking. For Lawson had scarcely commenced working when it ignited and a slight explosion followed. The weaving shed which contained two storeys of looms, one of spinning wheels and an upper storey, or attic, containing reels, was lit in its entirety by the main gas pipe near to which Lawson was working. Immediately the gas ignited the lights in the weaving shed

Alderman Edmund Birley – the mill ended up in his sole control

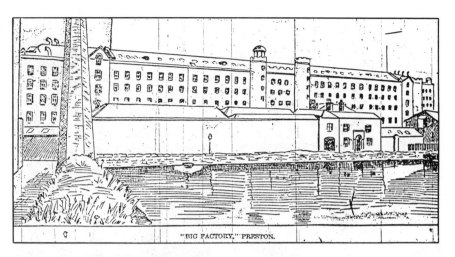

"BIG FACTORY," PRESTON.

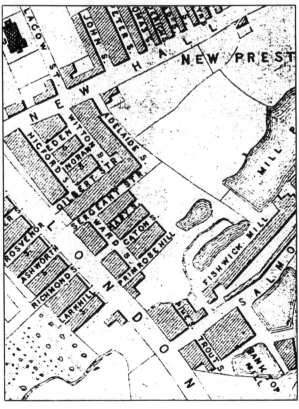

On a dark winter's morning in 1849 Thomas Lawson, a mill labourer, triggered a terrible tragedy

Marked as 'Fishwick Mill', the 'Big Factory' was off London Road

Inside the weaving shed the workers were unaware of the tragedy about to unfold

and the mechanics' shop went out, and the hands at once, and simultaneously, threw off the straps and this stopped the machinery, as it was impossible to attend properly to the work in the dark.

The machinery of the weaving shed was worked by an engine in a room called the East End Engine Room. The room contained two engines, one of 90 horse power and the other of 40 horse power. As soon as the hands employed at the weaving shed disconnected the looms from the motive power, greater velocity was given to the engine working it, the increased momentum given to the engine being at least treble what it was previously.

The engine-tenter, a man named John Cook, seeing the lights in the weaving shed go out and imagining the result, ran back to the engine house to turn off the stop valve, as he knew that there would be very soon a much greater pressure of steam than the engine could bear.

He ascended the steps leading from the lodge to the engine house, dashed past the boiler house and entering the room threw his arm over the valve to turn it. As he did so the flywheel from the smaller engine gave way and flew into upwards of thirty pieces, breaking down walls and massive iron rods and pillars, and strewing rubbish and wreckage in every direction.

When the flywheel, which was 16 feet in diameter and weighed 7 tons, flew into pieces a segment, upwards of 2 feet in length, struck the steam box of the smaller engine and broke it off. The unfortunate man's arm was across the box at the time and either the segment struck it or the pressure of the steam caught it, and it was forced completely from its socket. The floor where John Cook was standing was of flags and beneath it was the cold water cistern. A portion of the fly wheel crashed through the floor and the poor fellow was forced between the flooring into the engine bed.

Immediately on hearing the explosion, the workmen employed in the adjoining buildings ran to the spot to ascertain the injury done. The room was, however, so full of steam that for some time they were unable to enter it, or see what had occurred. Knowing that the engine-tenter was in the engine house, some of them shouted for him and at the third call, he answered, "I am here" with a moaning shout from the cistern. They promptly set about releasing him from his dreadful situation. It was only with great difficulty that they found the precise spot where the poor fellow lay, huddled up, and as he was too much injured to bear rough handling, they procured some remnants of cotton pieces and lowering them, they wrapped him in them and drew him up. His appearance was truly frightful, as he was severely scalded all over by the steam and his right arm had been entirely blown away.

Wrapping him tightly in the cotton remnants, they removed him carefully to his home in Salmon Street, just a few yards from the mill. Medical assistance had been quickly sent for by the mill manager and the man's wounds were dressed, and cotton applied to scalded parts. Although every attention was paid to him he died that same day around eight o'clock in the evening. The poor fellow, who remained sensible until almost the last moment, left behind a widow and eight children.

As John Cook was making a gallant attempt to prevent the disaster, another man, Henry Kirkham, the overlooker in the throttle room, also realised the danger. Entering the engine room from the opposite end, he proceeded to the throttle valve of the large engine and succeeded in turning it off. Then as he switched his attention to the other valve disaster struck him also. The force of the escaping steam impacted against him and he was flung back towards the entrance door. He was killed instantaneously, his skull being fractured, his legs broken and all over his head, body, legs and arms, he was most severely scalded.

Mr. Oddie, the manager of the mill was the first person to enter the engine room after the accident occurred, and as he stepped into the room with a lighted lamp in his hand, he discovered the dead body of Kirkham on the floor beside the door. It was apparent that the unfortunate young man had been struck by a portion of the fragmented flywheel and been subjected to the full force of the steam pressure. The body of Kirkham, who was about 23-years-old, was conveyed to his Pole Street home where his wife and young child were informed of his untimely end. When the inquests were held into the deaths of the two mill hands, the circumstances surrounding the tragedy were recounted.

Apparently the gas in the mill had frequently gone out and, in consequence the engine had 'run away', but never before had a serious accident occurred. Had John Cook been in his proper place, the engine house, he would have been able to react, as previously, to the situation. He had gone to the boiler house to collect some cotton waste for cleaning the engines, although strictly speaking, his duty was to remain in the engine room. Thomas Lawson was called, and he was asked to explain the incident that ignited the gas and led to the subsequent failure of the power supply. He told those gathered that in the first instance he had begun his work in the dark, but unable to see clearly, he had been forced to get a lamp.

The Coroner, Richard Palmer, Esquire, informed the Jury that they would be justified in returning a verdict of accidental death. After a few minutes consultation they informed the Coroner that they had reached such a verdict, but wished to add that they thought it was very improper for the man to have gone in search of gas with a light at that time on a winter's morning. The Coroner told them that he felt there was not that degree of culpable negligence which would enable them to return a verdict of manslaughter against Lawson. Adding that in his opinion Thomas Lawson should not have any blame attached to him. On the following Sunday afternoon the two victims of the fatal accident were interred in the churchyard of St. Paul's. The funeral and all other expenses being defrayed by Messrs. Swainson, Birley & Company.

Postscript

1. Prior to his death in March, 1895 Edmund Birley had for some years been the sole owner of the mill. Alderman Birley, who was Guild Mayor in 1882, having control of a mill that could boast 98,000 spindles.

2. In the 'Preston Guardian' in August, 1900 it was announced that the 'Big Factory' was to transfer from the Trustees of Messrs. Swainson, Birley and Co. to the ownership of Messrs. Horrockses, Crewsdon and Co. It was acknowledged that the 'Big Factory' had, during the nineteenth century, done much to build up the fame of Preston as a textile centre.

PRESTON WIDOW SENTENCED TO HANG

A PRESTON woman to hang was the outcome of a set of circumstances that occurred in the town in the year of 1898. The woman whose life was in the balance, was a Preston widow Isabella Cookson, and the sentence was passed after her trial in April, 1898, at Manchester Assizes.

The drama had begun on Thursday morning, 3rd March, when the Preston police discovered the body of a newly-born male child on the Frenchwood Tips. From enquiries made it transpired that the boy was the child of a single woman, aged 22, living in Pleasant Bank Place, Oxford Street. The girl was Phyllis Rosbottom who was living with her mother, Isabella Cookson, and during the early hours of that morning she had given birth to the child.

The cries of the newly-born infant had been heard by a neighbour who said she had heard a conversation in the adjoining house. The voice of a young woman breaking the stillness of the night with a cry of: "Oh! Mamma, Mamma don't. If you do you will never have any luck while you live. Don't do it, oh, don't." Then someone was heard to answer in an angry voice: "I will show you what I will do for it." To which a reply came: "If you do, Mamma I will drown myself." Five or ten minutes later the child's cries ceased, and someone was heard to leave by the front door and turn the corner of the street which led directly to the place where the body was found.

Within days Isabella Cookson appeared before the Magistrates in a crowded police court. She was charged with causing the death of the child. Her reply was: "I have done nothing of the kind." At that time her daughter was in Preston Infirmary and said to be progressing well from her traumatic ordeal. She had been at her work place, Moor Park Mill in St. George's Road the morning after the birth of her child. Accused of concealing the child's birth she had become distraught and placed in the Infirmary for care and observation.

After a further hearing Isabella Cookson was committed to stand trial for the alleged murder of the newly-born male child of her daughter. The trial took place on Friday 22nd April, before Mr. Justice Bigham. Mrs. Cookson, who was accompanied by a wardress from

Strangeways Gaol, was placed in the dock immediately the court opened. When challenged with the crime by the Clerk of the Assizes, she answered in a weak voice, "Not Guilty." The prisoner showed signs of dejection and her appearance was somewhat haggard and her cheeks flushed.

As the trial unfolded, neighbours recounted how they had heard strange noises from the Cookson household on the night in question. It was stated that the cries of the child, which had lasted 45 minutes, stopped all at once and that there had been the sound of blows consistent with the use of a stick.

What happened during the night was a matter of much speculation and the accused claimed the child had died and that she merely disposed of the body, to avoid any scandal.

One neighbour repeated a remarkable statement made to her by the accused on the morning of the child's discovery, recalling how Mrs. Cookson had said to her: "What do you think? I have been on Avenham this morning. At the bottom of the valley I saw a child. It was wrapped in flannel – good white flannel too. The child was dead."

The postmortem examination was discussed and it was stated that the child had definitely lived and death was due to exposure. Quizzed about the birth of the child without attendance of professional skill, Doctor Rigby declined to commit himself.

Finally, the daughter Phyllis Rosbottom was called and although the prosecution declined to question her, she was quizzed by the defence. Giving her evidence very intelligently, she stated that she had never told her mother about her condition and that when the child was born, Mrs. Cookson had been downstairs. When asked if she had been beaten by a stick or anything, she replied that her mother had never struck her nor put a hand upon her.

As the learned Counsel addressed the Jury the prisoner seemed acutely aware of her situation and was frequently in tears.

The defence Counsel stated how shame had come upon the prisoner's house, home and family and honestly believing the child to be dead, she had disposed of the body.

In his summing up the judge said the whole question was whether the child was alive and if the prisoner knew it. If Mrs. Cookson knew it was alive when she threw it away then no one could doubt that she intended the child should die. If this was so, he added, then the prisoner was undoubtedly guilty of murder.

The Counsel for the prosecution said there was an alternative verdict of manslaughter but His Lordship, Mr. Justice Bigham, felt that in his opinion such a verdict would be an improper one; the prisoner being either guilty of murder or nothing.

On returning into court the Jury gave a verdict of 'Guilty' with a recommendation to mercy. However, His Lordship proceeded to pass sentence of death on the Preston widow, remarking that the Jury's mercy plea should be forwarded to the proper quarter. The execution of Mrs. Cookson was fixed for 10th May.

Seven days later on 29th March, a communication was received from the Home Secretary. It stated that the death sentence was withdrawn and replaced by one of penal servitude for life.

ON TO DISASTER RUSHED THE MIDNIGHT EXPRESS

AT eight o'clock on Sunday evening, the 12th of July, 1896 the London and North Western Company's express train to Scotland left Euston Station. At Bletchley, Rugby and Crewe, the usual stoppages were made and at the last-mentioned place the customary division of the train took place. The first portion, consisting of the noted engines 'Shark' and 'Vulcan', two sleeping and four ordinary carriages, and a guard's van was despatched via Wigan and Preston for Aberdeen. Aboard were between 30 and 40 passengers, fewer than usual due to its leaving London on a Sunday evening.

At Wigan, the fourth stop of the journey, the usual examination of the wheels and springs was made prior to the long haul to Carlisle. The night was fine and clear and everything apparently favoured a fast run. Observers at Leyland station saw the Scotch Express thunder by at some 60 miles per hour, and within minutes it was approaching Preston station at speed.

As it passed through Preston station shortly after midnight, the guard's van lights had barely vanished from view, when the stillness of the night was broken by an indescribable noise. Immediately beyond the station were the diamond points, known as Dock Street points, and it was here that disaster occurred. The leading engine jumped off the rails at this point and crashed into the broadsiding which bordered the main roadway. The brakes were instantly applied and the heavy soil broken up by the engine helped to retard its progress. By great good fortune the engine came to a standstill just before it reached the brink of an embankment some 20ft. high.

The couplings of the coaches were wrenched and broken and the coaches themselves were overturned in all directions, some lying across and at right angles to the line, while one ended up beyond the foremost engine and was shattered against some heavy-laden stationary trucks. Sleepers were torn up and scattered and two telegraph poles were knocked down, severing communications.

The carriages were smashed in such a manner that it seemed impossible that the occupants could have escaped death or serious injury. Incredible, despite the carnage, the casualties were extremely

*The record-breaking engine
Vulcan sped through
Preston station and . . .*

*. . . on to the
notorious curve*

light, with one man killed and nine others injured. The dead man
was 20-year-old Donald Mavor, a stonemason from Aberdeen, who
had been travelling alone in a third class compartment. He was horribly mutilated, his skull being fractured and one arm wrenched from
the socket, while his legs and the other arm were badly fractured.
Despite immediate assistance from Preston station he expired before
he could be removed from the wreckage. Medical aid was given to
the injured passengers who were treated with every care by Drs.
Brown and Holden. Most of them were suffering from broken bones
or lacerations.

The breakdown gang worked throughout the night on the tan-
gled wreckage and eventually at two o'clock on the Monday afternoon the lines were relaid on the mail thoroughfare.

A pointsman in charge of the signal box overlooking the scene
of the accident blamed the abruptness of the curve for the derailment.
As the crash occurred everything became dark, with the gas all round,

even in the signal box, being cut off by the occurrence. He was consequently unable to see anything until officials from the station arrived with lanterns and set fire to some gathered heaps of debris.

An elderly gentleman from Ross-shire, whose appearance indicated that he had met with an uncommon experience, described his ordeal in the following manner -

"I travelled in the Inverness sleeping berth which adjoined the engines and I noticed, as we passed several of the points, that the train rocked considerably. As we approached Preston this became particularly noticeable, and I found that the velocity seemed to be much greater than usual when passing through Preston station. The train, immediately after, gave several jumps and with a premonition that a disaster was going to occur, I actually got up from my bed to put my boots on. Before I could get hold of them however, the train went off the lines, the lights went out and I was in darkness. Within seconds we came to a dead stop and I found myself with a mass of timber, the door and other carriage debris upon me. With everything shattered to pieces, it was not a matter of great difficulty to get out and I made my escape by taking things away piecemeal. It took me about ten minutes to free myself and I managed to do it without assistance, and with the exception of shaking, I don't think I am hurt. I was the first to escape and the scene I witnessed was a remarkable one with carriages toppled here and there, and cries echoing in the darkness from various carriages amid the debris."

Police Constable Woodacre of the Preston police force was one of the first on the scene and he gave a harrowing account of his experience -

"I was in Orchard Street when news was brought to me of the accident. When I arrived the first thing I did was to search the carriages and I came across the compartment where a man was said to be. I found him with his head through the window, and from all appearances the side of the carriage had fractured his back. Judging from the position in which I found him I came to the conclusion that he had laid down to sleep with his head in the direction of the window, and when the crash came he was thrown partly through it. He was scalped, completely scalped. We broke the end of the carriage with great difficulty, and with a saw we managed to get him out. He moved his hand which was the only sign of life I could see. We conveyed the body to the Station Master's room for there could be no doubt that life was extinct. At the mortuary I searched the body and found upon it an insurance ticket for £1,000, a railway ticket for Aberdeen, four half crowns, a purse, and a Geneva watch. Upon examination of the luggage we found a note in a handbag bearing the name Donald Mavor."

One of the rescuers related a tale of less tragic description. Hastening to one carriage from which it was evident the passengers had not escaped, he found the occupant to be a foreigner. The railway man made entrance to the compartment without ceremony, to awaken or assist the man as the case might be. The foreigner, however, mistook the intentions of his visitor. Coupling the overthrow of the express with the entry of the man, he thought the train had been 'held up'. Immediately, he grabbed his wallet from beneath his pillow and rushed towards his would-be rescuer with a fierce cry of "Hah! My money."

The railway man was seized by the throat with such violence that he thought he was in danger of being strangled. Fortunately, he escaped the man's clutches and eventually the foreigner realised what had occurred.

An engine cleaner who was working at the station at the time of the accident gave a graphic account of the crash.

"I heard the engines blowing off steam as they approached, and the train came along at a terrific pace. It's the one that does 105 miles in 105 minutes. They would be doing 50 miles per hour. Suddenly I saw a great blaze of light. I thought at first that it was a flash of lightning, but then I saw a great volume of flame and smoke, sparks and live coals. It was the engine 'Shark' that had had its chimney knocked off; it must have been by coming into collision with one of the telegraph poles down there. Then there was a horrible noise, sounding, while it lasted, for all the world like thunder, but somehow, on the still of the night air, even more terrible. You could not hear much of the passengers, even if they did scream, but it seemed to me that they were frightened into silence by the horrible din of the engines. I never saw such a scene in my life, and I never want to again."

An enquiry into the accident got underway on the Tuesday after the tragedy and it took place at the Park Hotel, Preston. A verdict of 'accidental death' was delivered on the man from Aberdeen killed in the crash. There was much discussion about the speed of the 'Scotch Express' on the fateful night.

In the summing up of the court of enquiry it was stated that the accident was brought about by the excessive rate of speed at which the train had been travelling. They did not however, consider the drivers were entirely at fault, but thought the distance from Wigan to Carlisle was too great for the time allowed for the train to cover it. It was stated that just a week before the 'Scotch Express' had made the run from Wigan to Carlisle, a distance of 105 miles, in 105 minutes.

It was recommended by the enquiry that the London and North Western Railway officers ensure that their bye-laws were strictly observed in the future.

THE TRAGIC HOMECOMING OF RACHAEL HART

THERE were in the town of Preston, during the Guild Week of 1882, more people than at any time during its previous history. Visitors came from the most varied parts, some from far away places. The enjoyment and great success of that Guild was enhanced by the delightfully fine weather which prevailed.

By custom the Guild Week gave many Prestonians the excuse they needed to return to the town of their birth. One such visitor in September, 1882 was Rachael Hart, who had spent her Preston childhood firstly in Edward Street and later in Poplar Street. Her parents, Mr. & Mrs. Leonard had earned their livelihood by owning a number of pigs and cultivating some garden land at the bottom of the Marsh. Eventually, her parents had tired of the daily toil and had emigrated to America, leaving Rachael and her brother, who set up in Preston as a clogger, to fend for themselves.

So it was that at the tender age of sixteen the then Rachael Leonard was courted and wedded by Edward Hart. He was an ambitious young man in the cotton trade and to further his career he moved his family to Pendleton, near Manchester. Within little time he was in the responsible position of mill manager, well able to provide for a wife and the three children, two daughters and a son, which she bore him.

The couple did not, however, enjoy a lifetime's togetherness and after some twenty years a misunderstanding occurred which caused them to separate. From the time of parting from her husband, Mrs. Hart contrived to get a living by various means, working chiefly as a weaver in Lancashire towns. In her wanderings she had frequently

On the last night of her life, Rachael Hart visited the New Britannia Inn in Heatley Street

visited Preston and on a previous visit had spent almost two years working at a factory in Back Lane.

The next visit was the one in Guild Week, 1882 when, on the opening day, she turned up in Hope Street and gained lodgings with a Mrs. Fawcett. By now in her mid forties, and after ten years of separation, she had earned the reputation of being of loose character.

From the start of her stay she had nothing to eat except what meagre food Mrs. Fawcett, who was herself in indigent circumstances, provided for her. This being in marked contrast to the sumptuous feasts and banquets partaken of by the titled gentry and dignitaries, who honoured the town with their presence at the Guild celebrations.

Rachael Hart was certainly no quitter and in the week following the Guild she visited a number of local mills seeking employment. The cotton trade was enjoying a boom period and on the middle Saturday of the month she succeeded in gaining employment as a four-loom weaver at Mr. Hawkins' mill in Adelphi Street.

Having obtained new lodgings at Simpson's Brow with a Mr. and Mrs. Day, she went with them that night to the public houses in Heatley Street, intent on celebrating her new employment, which was arranged to start the following Monday morning. After visiting the New Britannia Inn the three of them spent from nine to ten o'clock in the Pack Horse Inn. At that time Mr. and Mrs. Day set off for home, while Rachael, who had other plans, made her way towards the town centre.

The same night two men, William McDermott, a private in the King's Own Lancashire Regiment stationed at Fulwood Barracks and his friend, Thomas Clarkson, a clog iron maker, were on one of their regular peregrinations in the town. They did in fact visit numerous public houses and by eleven o'clock they were more drunk than sober. At the time William McDermott suggested that the pair of them should go to the home of his mother and sister, which was situated in a yard off Friargate.

To get to that place it was necessary for them to pass through the area known as Hardman's Yard. When they got into the passageway they observed at one side a couple engaged in conversation. On getting closer, William McDermott recognised the woman as Rachael Hart and said to her, "What are you doing here?" Both being of an intemperate nature they had often met in the various drinking establishments they frequented.

From her bedroom window, overlooking Hardman's Yard, milliner Nancy Garth saw the soldier attacking the woman

The man who was in her company took exception at McDermott's interference and within an instant had struck him a violent blow. Then, before the soldier could recover, he turned on his heels and fled into the night along the dimly-lit passageway.

Rachael Hart was none too happy at the unwelcome intrusion and she made use of some strong expressions as McDermott rose to his feet and then, as he approached her, she hit out at him. This enraged McDermott who gave her a violent blow with his fist upon the head, in consequence of which she was thrown against some shutters and afterwards fell to the ground. Despite the force of the blow she got up and he again struck her several times, knocking her down again. When she was on the floor he kicked her about the legs until eventually Thomas Clarkson interfered by grabbing hold of McDermott's coat collar, saying, "You have done enough; for God's sake, come away."

While all this was going on Nancy Garth, a milliner of 22 Friargate was just entering her bedroom, which had a window that opened on to Hardman's Yard. She heard the screaming and the shouting and observed McDermott in the process of attacking the woman. When the struggling was over she saw the two men hurry out of the yard.

Miss Garth went immediately down to the yard, by which time P.C. William Roucroft was at the scene. He had found Rachael Hart lying against the wall of the house, with her feet bent under her. The constable took hold of her round the wrists and observed she was still alive. She appeared to be bleeding from the mouth and within five minutes she had stopped breathing.

Her body was at once taken to the mortuary where local surgeon Dr. Hart made an examination. His diagnosis showed that the woman had been in an unhealthy condition. Besides the injuries to shins and head caused by her assailant, he also commented on a couple of old bruises. His examination revealed that the membrane of the brain was very much congested and there was a large clot of blood in the base of it. The lungs, kidneys and stomach were congested and the left ventricle of the heart was swollen.

His analysis was that death was caused by an effusion of blood on the brain and he believed that the amount of mischief on the brain could certainly not have come on that night. The brain, he concluded, was softer than it ought to be and also very much disordered.

The search for McDermott was only a short one. He was found at his mother's house, 8 Mellings Yard. He was lying on a bed in the kitchen, with his trousers, shirt and stockings on. When he was charged, he said, "Murdered a woman! Good God, good God."

On Tuesday the 19th of September, 1882 an Inquest was held at the Police Court and, as a result, McDermott was committed for trial at Manchester Assizes, on a charge of manslaughter. The Jury also expressed their disgust at the conduct of Thomas Clarkson, who they said, had stood by whilst the poor unfortunate woman was kicked to death.

When the Manchester Winter Assizes took place at the beginning of November, 1882 the eighteen-year-old William McDermott was greatly helped in his cause by the testimony of Dr. Hart, the surgeon from Winckley Square.

He told the gathering that the whole organ of the brain had been in a state of advanced disease. Life under any circumstances, he considered, would not have been prolonged for any length of time.

In conclusion he felt that the violence of the prisoner had nothing to do with the death of the poor woman.

Subsequently, the Jury returned a verdict of 'Not Guilty' and His Lordship, in discharging the prisoner, said the assault had been most cowardly and a cruel one, which anyone entrusted to wear Her Majesty's uniform, ought to be ashamed of.

For Racheal Hart the end had been a brutal one, even if only slightly premature, if the medical analysis was accurate. Certainly though, William McDermott had only escaped a long prison sentence by ironic fortune. For one so young he was already well known to the police for his drinking and gambling habits and the impression was that Mr. Justice Day had been reluctant to see him walk free from the court of justice.

ISABELLA'S CHILD WAS SLOWLY DYING

IN the month of April, 1891 Isabella Torbett, of Sedgwick Street, a 37-year-old married woman, gave birth to her fourth child, a daughter, which she named Margaret. The new arrival was a frail and delicate child and after a short time Mrs. Torbett put the infant out to be nursed by a Mrs. Adamson.

The baby was in her care for six weeks and while in her charge it did very well. The mother, however, took it away and within a few more weeks the child's health deteriorated and gave cause for concern. So much so that Mrs. Adamson was again asked to take care of the infant. Again, she nursed it with tender care and affection and again, the infant's health improved.

By Christmas, 1891 the child's mother wanted her infant back and it was agreed that she should take her daughter home. Unfortunately, the mother was somewhat addicted to drink, and the infant did not receive the attention it required. Yet again the baby's health fell back and the mother resorted to Mrs. Adamson's aid on a number of occasions. Her nursing skills were called upon as the mother lapsed into drinking bouts.

Isabella Torbett had been at home since Christmas, having left her job as a weaver, but her care for the child had not increased. Her husband, George Torbett, who worked long hours to provide for his family, had returned home on more than one occasion and found the child in its cradle unattended.

On one day in February, 1892 the mother took the infant, which was suffering from a very bad cold, to Mrs. Adamson's house at six-thirty in the morning. Having left the little thing there, she did not return for it until eleven o'clock that night. When the mother called to collect the infant, Mrs. Adamson refused to hand the child over, as she could see that the mother was somewhat the worse for drink. She kept the infant all night, sitting by the fire with it.

About that time an Inspector for the Prevention of Cruelty to Children visited Mrs. Torbett's home and, finding a worrying state of affairs, cautioned her that unless she attended better to the child, she would be held responsible by the law.

The woman though took no notice of the warning and continued in her bad ways. The next day she left her home, took the child with her, left it at a house in Salter Street and went out drinking with some women friends. That day she never returned to her home or to collect her child. In fact, it was six o'clock the following morning when she called to get the baby. On a cold winter's morning she took it through the streets to her house, clothed only in a chemise, and when they arrived home the child was almost stone cold.

For a number of weeks a similar pattern of behaviour persisted and various neighbours and acquaintances had the infant left in their care, while the mother frequented the beer houses of the town. Her unbalanced lifestyle and general disregard for the infant had the effect of worsening the child's health and, as February drew to a close, so did the baby's life.

Perhaps one day more than any other stretched the durability of the child more than was humanly possible. That day was the 26th of February, 1892, a day on which Isabella Torbett agreed to meet a man called William Marshall in the Coachmakers' Arms in Egan Street. She met him with the child in her arms and, as they sat drinking, the landlady of the public house called Mrs. Torbett's attention to the condition of the youngster. It seemed to be very ill, filled with cold, and in such a state that it was dangerous for it to be out.

The landlady told the mother this, warmed the child by the fire and gave it some milk and tea. She then told Mrs. Torbett to take the child home. The mother ignored the advice and went almost immediately to the Sitting Goose public house, situated on North Road. Once again she and Marshall sat themselves down and started to drink. The landlady there also spoke to the mother as to the condition of the baby, telling her to go home and get a doctor to call. Upon the landlady's insistence they eventually left and Mrs. Torbett took the child home. No doctor was called for, although she did purchase a bottle of medicine on the way home.

A bottle of medicine could not halt the infant's decline after months of habitual neglect and ill treatment. When Mrs. Torbett entered the house, her husband complained at her keeping the child out and at her drunken state. She told him she had been out with William Marshall and that there was nothing wrong and the child was all right.

The husband observed that the infant appeared to be very weak, but did nothing except see that the youngster was placed in its cradle.

At about four o'clock the following morning his wife awoke him saying, "George, I think the child is dying." Within another hour the baby had expired.

At the inquest, Mr. Torbett told the Coroner of his wife's drinking habit, and her increased neglect of the baby. He stated that he had frequently spoken to her about her conduct, but she did not appear to take any notice of what he said.

The general opinion was that the mother's conduct had hastened the child's death and consequently Isabella Torbett was committed to take her trial at Lancaster Assizes.

Within days considerable sensation was caused in the town when it became known that William Marshall, one of the principal witnesses in the case against the woman Torbett, had committed suicide at his home in Morgan Street.

It was revealed that Marshall had been in depressed spirits since losing his job three months previously. According to his wife Jane, the 46-year-old Marshall had been suffering from sleeplessness since before Christmas.

On the day of his death, his wife had left their home at eight o'clock leaving her husband in bed. The night before he had asked her if, on rising next morning, she would not disturb him, as he would like to try and lie on a bit longer.

When Jane Marshall returned to their Morgan Street home at ten thirty that morning she found her husband hanging in the back kitchen from a hook in the ceiling. He had all his clothes on, except for his jacket. It appeared that he had climbed up a pair of steps, fixed a rope and then kicked the steps away, leaving his feet dangling two feet off the kitchen floor.

A piercing scream from Mrs. Marshall had alerted the neighbours and one of them quickly cut the body down. Medical assistance was soon on hand in the form of Dr. Dunn, but when he examined the man he was quite dead.

An inquest was held at the Albert Hotel in Ribbleton Lane and the jury found that William Marshall had committed suicide while temporarily insane.

The trial of Isabella Torbett took place at Lancaster Assizes on Friday 11th March, 1892 before Lord Chief Justice Coleridge. She was charged with the manslaughter of her daughter at Preston.

The prosecution outlined the catalogue of neglect and related the various instances that suggested the mother's disregard for her infant's well-being. Written testimony from the deceased man William Marshall was also used to emphasise the woman's apparent disregard for her child's welfare.

The Defence Counsel claimed that the prosecution had failed to show criminal neglect on the part of the mother. She might have been a drunken woman, he admitted, but that would not make her Guilty of hastening the death of her child.

Lord Chief Justice Coleridge – when he announced her sentence, Isabella Torbett fainted into the arms of the prison wardens

The Jury, after half an hour's absence, returned with a verdict of 'Guilty', but with a recommendation for mercy due to the child having a long-standing disease of the lungs.

When His Lordship prepared to pass sentence, he said that he would mark the sense of neglect shown by the mother not as heavily as originally intended, but sufficiently strong to show other folk that they must not hasten the death of their children. Isabella Torbett was then informed that she must go into penal servitude for three years. On hearing the sentence the woman cried out "Oh, Merciful Father," and then fainted into the arms of the prison warder

*   *   *

A couple of weeks later a trial took place in Dublin where Annie Mary Montagu was found 'Guilty' of manslaughter of her child, Helen Mary, aged three. Her death having been caused, or accelerated, by acts of wanton cruelty. The mother was recommended to mercy on the ground that the act of cruelty, or so-called punishment, was committed under a mistaken sense of duty. Mr. Justice Murphy observed that nothing could warrant the heartless course which the woman had pursued, and sentenced her to twelve months imprisonment.

As a result the 'Preston Chronicle' newspaper of the second Saturday in April, 1892 carried an editorial highlighting the two manslaughter cases, and the punishments meted out to the respective criminals.

In the matter of education and social status the newspaper pointed out the women were at the opposite ends of the pole. Isabella

41

Torbett was a poor, miserable, uneducated creature, the wife of a working man, whose earnings were but scanty at the best. Whereas Annie Mary Montagu, whose very name bespoke of superiority of birth, was the wife of a gentleman of influence and position. She resided at Coleraine House, Coleraine and was surrounded by servants. The offence with which the two women were charged was the same, yet manslaughter is a crime of extremely varying degrees. Ranging, according to circumstances, from an offence closely bordering on murder to almost justifiable homicide.

Hence, the newspaper reminded the readers of the details of the two cases. Isabella Torbett, a poor, miserable woman, had fallen into degrading habits of intemperance and to satisfy her craving for drink had gone out at all hours, taking her weakly, sickly infant with her, on occasions remaining away from home all night. The child had got little food and no care, with drink making the mother reckless of her duties. Owing to the systematic neglect the slender thread of debilitated infant life had snapped. However, beyond the deprivation of food and nourishment, there was no evidence of actual violence or physical cruelty on the part of the mother.

As for Annie Mary Montagu she was a woman moving in high circles, possessed of ample means to maintain her family in comfort and luxury. She was possessed of more than ordinary intelligence and had a capacity for weighing the consequences of her action, which Isabella Torbett was scarcely deemed to have. From the revolting volumes of evidence submitted the facts in Mrs. Montagu's case were as follows.

The unfortunate child of three had, up to the 13th of February, 1892 been healthy and hearty. On that day she was punished by being deprived of her breakfast for being late in coming downstairs. At lunchtime on the same day she was for some trifling offence locked in a small, dark, unventilated room.

Shortly after she was visited by her mother, who added to the penalties already suffered by the little prisoner by binding her arms behind her with a stocking, which was fastened to a ring in the wall by a piece of string. At five o'clock the child, who had not been seen for three hours, was found dead.

According to the woman's own statement the child when found was bent forward and the stocking was round her neck. Medical testimony showed that pressure on the windpipe had probably been the immediate cause of death.

The facts were not disputed as far as the accused woman was concerned, but her eminent Counsel urged that the worst that could be said of the woman was that her ideas of the discipline of children had led her into a grievous mistake. The Jury of course, found her 'Guilty', but also recommended her to mercy.

According to the 'Preston Chronicle', the cruelty she had practised on that child had been not merely wanton, but vilely deliberate, and the suggestion that it could be excused on a plea of duty was puerile nonsense.

The paper was not suggesting that the punishment given to Isabella Torbett was unusually harsh, or more than the crime deserved, but if her punishment was just, then what could be said of that inflicted on Mrs. Montagu?

The reality was that when the accomplished, intelligent, well-to-do woman had completed her sentence for her heinous crime, the poorer sister from Preston would still have nearly two years to serve, amid the hardships of a penal settlement.

DESTINED TO WALK THE STREETS OF PRESTON

D URING the second half of the year 1888 the newspapers of Preston, like those in all the provincial towns and cities, carried banner headlines that reported a seemingly endless list of tragedies in the East End of London. Grimness and misery was portrayed as murders and mutilations occurred all too frequently.

The victims were generally from the lower classes, and were women who paraded the streets and alleyways of Whitechapel, earning their living as prostitutes. With each killing the fear increased, yet the women had no alternative but to continue their perilous profession.

It was the time in history when the person known later as 'Jack the Ripper' roamed the streets, and from the end of August to the beginning of November, five murders were committed that were believed to be the work of that undetected killer.

The outcome of all this tragedy and terror was that the public became all too aware of the plight of the prostitutes. They gained a great deal of sympathy from all quarters and it was generally recognised that a large proportion were poor, poverty stricken and dejected creatures who had been dealt a less fortunate hand.

Of course Preston was no exception and it had its fair share of women who walked the streets. While they were a long way from the alleyways frequented by the 'Ripper', their situation nonetheless became regarded as a dangerous and unenviable one. There was a genuine concern for the fallen sisterhood that continued long after the headlines of 1888 had paled into distant memory.

A typical example of the concern was expressed a few days before Christmas in 1890. On a wet, miserable night just after eleven o'clock a local industrialist arrived at Preston station from Blackburn. Business had detained him later than usual and as he alighted from the train he looked forward to a pleasant fireside and wholesome supper, for he had hardly eaten anything since early morning.

Leaving the station along Butler Street he was soon onto Fishergate. Walking briskly along he was almost level with the Theatre Tavern, when he was accosted by a well dressed female. He stopped and spoke to her and a few moments sufficed to show him that he was in the company of a girl of the streets.

Low though she may have sunk there was an indefinable something in her appearance that excited his curiosity, and which prompted him to conversation. His new-found companion walked alongside him and displayed a vivacious exterior, frequently breaking her remarks with a peculiar laugh that outwardly expressed gaiety.

At this point the woman had assumed the man was receptive to her advances and she was somewhat taken aback when he began to enquire how she had ended up on the streets. She resented his enquiries, thinking him impertinent and after apologising for stopping him, the woman bade him farewell.

The man however, was not so easily shaken off and placing his hand gently on her arm he continued to quiz her about her past. Before him he saw a fellow creature, a cultured woman, who began to reveal with all sincerity a tale of harrowing depth.

As her story unfolded, tears firstly sparkled her long dark eyelashes and then began to stream down a hopeless-looking and paint-begrimed face. She told of a dead mother; of an unrequited love; of a cruel husband and a still more cruel father. Blessed with a tolerably good education, she had lost her mother when still young. Her father took little interest in her and she was practically left to choose her own career.

She met, admired and then loved a gay gallant, who wooed and won her, hoping for the gold which he believed the father would bestow on his daughter.

He reckoned though without his host, for when the marriage ceremony had been performed, it was found, too late, that the father had recognised the mercenary motives of his daughter's husband, and declined to acknowledge him.

In fact, the old man, unknown to his daughter, had intended her for another sphere of life than the one she had chosen. Telling the newly-wedded pair that – "As they had made their bed, so they must lie," turning them adrift without a shilling. The husband had not been used to work, and subsisted chiefly upon a small pittance allowed him by an old uncle.

Soon after the wedding, this uncle died and, in the absence of a Will, the eldest son claimed the property and refused to continue his father's benevolence. Poverty thus stared them in the face, and in the course of time a baby was born to share its unhappy parents' misery.

The young mother stayed at home repining and the husband's once much vaunted love was being tested. Eventually he upbraided his young wife for his disappointment respecting her father's money and with callous indifference packed his bags and left her.

From that day she never heard from him. Deserted, lonely and friendless, and almost without shelter, as her landlady had intimated that she could not be boarded for nothing, this virtuous young mother went to her father's house. She sought food and a home for herself and child, but her father sent her from his door, telling her to take her brat and go away. So away she went nestling her child to her bosom.

Though she was worn and wan through want, her face bore traces of loveliness, and laid her open to strong temptations. For a time she withstood them and refused to sell her honour for a price. Too proud to seek aid from her parent's friends, she was at length driven to theft. For this she was imprisoned. On regaining her liberty she left the town where she was known and made her way to Preston.

Here she was met and sympathised with by women who soon perverted the already broken spirit into their own dark ways of living. In a few days she found herself in the hands of the Preston police. In the charge room at the police station, before being removed to a cell, she hugged her baby to her breast and then handed it to someone she knew would care for it, giving instructions for its removal to friends of her former days.

She wished the child to be far removed from her own future life of sin and that night she pleaded with her Maker to preserve her offspring from the fate which had befallen her. Her circumstances had forced her on a downward course, and in the years that followed no vice or scene of shame eluded her as she mixed with the denizens of Preston's slums.

Such was the tale of sorrow gleaned by the businessman on that wretchedly wet night before Christmas in 1890, as he paraded Fishergate, with this strangely chosen companion. Before parting, he spoke hopefully to her; tried to turn her thoughts and aspirations into purer channels. He told her of a possible brighter future and half promised to secure friends to take an interest in her welfare.

To all of his remarks she shook her head, and murmured, "Too late, too late. I am much obliged to you, sir, but society will never recognise me again." She then hurried away, as if fearful to stay another moment, and she was soon lost to sight in the shadow of Preston's Parish Church, off to rejoin her companions of the streets.

As the man returned to his home the woman's words "Society will never recognise me" rang in his ears. Had society done its duty by this poor outcast, he wondered, and were scores of others destined to follow her unenviable path? His hope was that a helping hand would be stretched out to fallen sisterhood and a generous loving sympathy extended to those in need.

So affected was he by his chance encounter, that he was compelled to pen a letter to the 'Preston Chronicle' in which he recounted his experience. In it he appealed for all to show a greater understanding. He was particularly complimentary towards that remarkable organisation, The Salvation Army. His hope was that in the New Year the people of the town would welcome General Booth's 'Slum Sisters' as they attempted to raise the fallen from the path of perdition.

DARING DIAMOND ROBBERY IN FRIARGATE

ONE of the most familiar and popular tradesmen in nineteenth-century Preston was watchmaker Thomas Yates. In the middle of 1848 he was presented with a silver medal for his design of a Dead-Beat Lever watch.

At the age of sixteen he had arrived in Preston from his birthplace in Goosnargh and been apprenticed to a local watchmaker. Five years before his patent watch design he had commenced business at 159 Friargate as a watchmaker and jeweller. From his Friargate shop he served the people of the town and when not at business he served the cause of the town's Methodists. A staunch teetotaller he often said that he had never drunk, nor paid, for a glass of intoxicating liquor in his life.

A quiet, plodding worker, he was not the sort to be showy or to seek attention, but in December, 1882 an incident at his Friargate shop made him the focus of local interest. On the second Friday of the month, shortly after five o'clock, his young assistant departed leaving Mr. Yates alone in the shop. As he prepared to conclude the business of the day, the shop door was opened and in walked a stout-built man, dressed in a dark overcoat and wearing a muffler.

On entering he left the shop door open and, on advancing to the counter, asked the elderly Mr. Yates to show him some gem rings. Despite feeling that the man was rather a rough looking character and not the sort who usually purchased jewellery, Mr. Yates took down from one of the shelves a small case containing 30

Watchmaker and jeweller Thomas Yates was alone in his Friargate shop when the mysterious stranger entered the premises

rings, some set with diamonds others with rubies, emeralds, sapphires and pearls.

The man, who was being watched very closely by the jeweller, placed one of the gem rings on a finger and then in the next instant he grabbed the whole case of rings and darted for the open door. Due to his advancing years Mr. Yates was unable to leap the counter and by the time he had reached the shop door the thief was out of sight.

The incident caused the upmost of excitement and one gentleman recalled seeing two possible accomplices outside the shop. While another saw three men dash up and then down again from a blind passage further down Friargate.

It seemed that the young lad who assisted Mr. Yates had passed the man on his way out of the shop and from him and Mr. Yates, a description of the thief was pieced together by the police. It was reckoned the man was about 30 years of age, of sallow complexion with dark mutton chop whiskers and a short moustache.

The town's detective force were soon making enquiries and with the robbery haul being worth in the region of £500 the crime was regarded as a major one. Information of the offence was at once forwarded to the police in different parts of the country, together with details of the stolen gem rings.

Subsequent enquiries led the police to believe that the man at the centre of the raid had visited a pawnshop in Back Lane the previous night. The pawnbroker recalling a man who answered to the police description, having been on his premises with another man.

A 19th-century advertisement by the hightly-regarded local jeweller.

49

There was also a report that a mysterious stranger had spent a couple of nights at a Temperance Hotel in Butler Street. Throughout his stay the man had conducted himself in a suspicious manner.

In truth, there was a certain amount of vagueness in the information available to the police and despite the intense activity of the detective force, it was felt the thieves may well have left the town. The feeling being that they could have boarded a train at the railway station before the police were able to place a watch on the comings and goings from that place.

A week later though, it was reported that Detective Inspector Brown had made what was considered to be an important arrest in connection with the robbery. A man in his mid-thirties, of dark complexion with side whiskers and a moustache, was being questioned by the Preston police. Despite the similarities in description to the wanted man, no one was able to positively identify him as the person who robbed the jeweller's shop in Preston.

The man was, however, wanted elsewhere and before the week was out he was handed over to the Stockport police. They wanted him in connection with the theft of nine watches from a jeweller's shop in their town at the beginning of December.

The scale of the robbery was reflected in the Chief Constable's Annual Report in November, 1883 which showed that during the year the total value of property stolen was £675.

Thomas Yates soon recovered from his ordeal and despite his substantial loss continued to trade from his Friargate shop. When he died in February, 1890, aged 79, the newspaper headline read 'Death of the Oldest Tradesman in Town' – for 47 years he served the town from his jeweller's premises. To this day the name Thomas Yates adorns a Preston shop, but now the premises are in the Market Place.

Thomas Yates' name still adorns a shop in the Market Place

MAKING MISCHIEF WITH A COFFIN

UNLIKE the present day, the people of the mid-nineteenth century did not celebrate Hallowe'en with the commercially orientated ferocity of our time. Nonetheless, if opportunity presented itself there were those who, with mischief in mind, would set out to exploit the fears of the fainthearted.

So it was in the autumn of 1858, when the season once again turned to talk of witches, demons, boggarts and other fearsome apparitions, that two youths came by chance upon a discarded coffin. The lads, Richard Forshaw aged 19, and Robert Mawdsley, two years his junior, resided in the rural area known as Hoole, not many miles from Preston. Aware of the local superstitions, and in particular the fears of the younger element, they hatched a plot developed from their mischievous nature.

The youths knew of the apprehension amongst a group of local girls who had been told the tale of the 'boggart' that lay in wait on the turnpike road to Liverpool, in the stretch just past the Primitive Methodist Chapel, in Hoole. They also knew that daily the girls would walk along the road to their homes, after finishing their shift at the nearby mill of Mr. McKean. Consequently, on the last Friday before Hallowe'en in 1858, in the gathering dusk of an autumn evening, they carried their newly-acquired casket along the turnpike road until they reached the spot where the 'boggart' was believed to reside.

Placing the coffin in the middle of the highway, they attached a length of string to one of the handles and Mawdsley, with the other end of the string in his hand, concealed himself in the hedge which ran along one side of the road. Then his partner in mischief, hid himself in the ditch on the other side of the road, with instructions to make a fearful noise as the coffin moved.

The youths had timed their prank to perfection, as no sooner had they concealed themselves than they heard the chatter of their intended victims as they came within earshot.

To their horror, as they passed the Primitive Methodist Chapel, the girls observed the coffin lying in the road. As they approached it, the coffin appeared to rattle and shake, and a terrifying hollow sound seemed to emanate from within. It was too much for the innocent and impressionable youngsters to bear and, almost in unison the girls let out a series of piercing screams and turning on their heels dashed back down the turnpike road. Much to their relief not far behind them on the road had been Joseph Gill, a steam-loom weaver of their acquaintance, and soon he was besieged by half a dozen fearful and frightened young girls. A couple of them were visibly trembling, and they were all happy to cling on to him as he attempted to calm them down.

Only after he had reassured them that the incident must have been an elaborate prank, did they agree to continue their journey. As they once again approached the spot where the coffin lay, they saw the two youths in the process of raising it up to their shoulders. Not surprisingly Joseph Gill had a few choice words to say to the pair, but they made no response as they moved along.

Amongst the group of girls was Martha Spencer, aged thirteen, who appeared to have been more frightened than the rest of the party. When she got home that Friday evening she complained of being frightened by the coffin to her father, John Spencer, who was a handloom weaver. Despite her obvious distress, she ate her supper and retired to bed at the usual hour of ten o'clock. The following morning she rose early, ate her breakfast and went off to work. When she got there she complained of feeling unwell to her workmates, but conscious of her duties, remained until her shift finished at two o'clock.

On her return home her mother, Mary Spencer, had prepared her dinner for her, which she ate with little relish. The meal over, she stood by the fire in a subdued state prompting her mother to enquire "Martha, what ails thee?" The daughter replied that she had been poorly all day and promptly sat down by the fire and fell asleep.

She remained in that position until seven o'clock when her mother persuaded her to go to bed. That night was to be a troubled one in the Spencer house, as the daughter was overcome by sickness. She began to vomit water and blood at regular intervals, and by dawn her condition had deteriorated. In great distress she was moaning and groaning continually and her teeth were tightly clenched as her suffering intensified.

The distraught parents sent for Mr. Hunt, the local surgeon, but before he could do anything for the girl she died. The girl had always appeared healthy and happy and at once a connection was drawn between her frightful experience on the Friday night and her sudden demise.

On the following Monday evening, Miles Myres, the coroner from Preston, held an inquest at the house of William Sutton, in Much Hoole. Several witnesses were called and they recalled the events of the previous Friday, and the circumstances surrounding the girl's death.

One witness was a shoemaker, called Henry Hunt, who had heard the screams of the girls and who on meeting up with them later had noticed how frightened they were. He also told the gathering that he had seen Richard Forshaw in the Rose and Crown at Much Hoole on the night after the incident and said to him, "You are a bonny fellow to go and frighten children so." To which Forshaw had replied that they were only doing it for a lark.

Towards the close of the inquest Preston surgeon, Mr. W. Howitt, reported on the postmortem examination he had carried out on the deceased. He had found the cause of death to be rupture of the gall bladder, and extravasation of bile over the external surface of the intestines. The rupture had, he stated, existed for some little time, but he could not tell how long and the probable cause of the rupture might have been the fright she had received on the Friday. However, if the rupture had taken place on the Friday, he did not think that the girl could have eaten her meals as described by her parents. He therefore thought the probability was that she had been suffering from fright until the Saturday and that the rupture then took place. The fright probably being the exciting cause which produced the rupture.

The surgeon's testimony complete, the inquest Jury retired and when they returned they delivered a verdict of Manslaughter against Richard Forshaw and Robert Mawdsley. The two apprentice wheel-wrights were present at the inquest and they were immediately taken into custody, being committed for trial at Lancaster on a coroner's warrant. The frightful and heartless prank had created a great deal of interest and when it was reported in the 'Preston Chronicle', the headline simply said 'A GIRL FRIGHTENED TO DEATH'.

For four traumatic months the youths remained incarcerated, left to dwell upon the fate that awaited them for the frightful and heartless joke that had gone horribly and tragically wrong.

Lancaster's ancient castle had, down the centuries, been soaked in the tragedies of those who dealt in witchcraft and the dealings of the darker side of life, and the youths reflected repentantly on their harrowing Hallowe'en activity.

Eventually, in the middle of February 1859, Mr. Justice Willes opened the Lancaster Spring Assizes and amongst the cases put before the Grand Jury, was the bill for manslaughter by the two youths. It was a case, he observed, of the melancholy kind and he felt that after carefully looking into the matter, it was not one which amounted to manslaughter. It was proper, he thought, that the prisoners had been sent to trial, and he hoped that their committal to gaol would have the effect of deterring others from frightening girls in a similar way. It was purely an act of thoughtlessness and not one to warrant a verdict of manslaughter.

By His Lordship's directions the Grand Jury ignored the bill for manslaughter and when the youths appeared in the Crown Court, he gave them a lecture on the impropriety of their conduct. He told them they were guilty of a very thoughtless act in frightening a girl to death, and he hoped that they would not on any occasion repeat the offence. He did not wish to have them branded as felons, but it must be borne in mind that if any such occurrence should happen again, they would be severely punished.

Upon His Lordship's instructions, a verdict of 'Not Guilty' was delivered, and two very relieved young men were discharged.

AN AWFUL END FOR ALICE KNOWLES

'SHOCKING MURDER IN PRESTON, A WOMAN KICKED TO DEATH' read the headline in the Preston Guardian on Wednesday, November 21st, 1888. It then went on to inform readers of another sad murder which had been added to the criminal annals of Preston.

The killing involved Robert Knowles, a stout young fellow aged 32, and his wife Alice, who was some twelve months his junior. The couple resided in a lobby off Aughton Street, one of the thoroughfares between North Road and Lancaster Road. On the Tuesday evening when his wife had not returned home by ten o'clock the husband, who followed the occupation of pork butcher, went in search of her.

He found her, as he suspected he would, at a house in Westmorland Street, the home of William Windle and his family. When he entered the house his wife was seated in front of the fire with Mrs. Windle and somewhat impatiently he asked: "Look here, are you not coming home?" His wife made some muttered remark to which Robert Knowles replied by giving her a hard clout. It was enough to send his wife tumbling from her chair landing on her right side on the flagged floor. He was in a violent temper, infuriated by the fact his wife had been drinking all day. As she lay on the floor he aimed a single kick at her head. On his feet were iron clogs and the blow was sufficient to render his wife unconscious. Apparently unaware of the gravity of his actions, Knowles sat down in an armchair.

In the house at the time of the incident, was also the couple's eight-year-old daughter, Lizzie Ann Knowles, who was a horrified witness to the tragic event. She was the only living child of their marriage of several years, which had been traumatic, due to the loss in childhood of three or four other children.

With Alice Knowles laid on the floor, Mrs. Windle left the house to visit the local cook's shop to get Robert Knowles and the girl something to eat. Knowles followed her and paid for the food. They then returned to the house and to their surprise found the woman still laying motionless. Knowles then remarked: "Aye, she's dead enough." Medical aid was immediately sent for but the poor woman's life was at an end. The later conclusion being that death had been caused by the blow to the head which resulted in a blood clot at the base of the brain.

The room in which the body was found presented a wretched appearance. It was stated that Mrs. Knowles had been drinking during the day and that at the time of the fatal attack on his wife, Mr. Knowles was 'fresh in drink'.

When the police arrived, Knowles seemed utterly unable at first to realise what he had done. He quietly submitted to being taken into custody to the police station and placed in a cell.

When the inquest was held the following day, one of the first to give evidence was Alice Knowles' sister, Ann Scowcroft, the wife of Thomas Scowcroft, a hawker, of Spring Gardens. She told the hearing that her deceased sister, when in employment, was a weaver, but lately she had not done any work. She and her husband lived together but were not on good terms, although she had never complained of ill-usage by him. Her sister had taken drink in excess for several years and unfortunately had become a very drunken woman. Her husband was a hard-working man who had always appeared to be a kind and affectionate husband. Many a time the husband had remarked to her that, "If she would only let that drink alone, how comfortable we should be."

Ellen Windle was next to give evidence and besides recounting the tragic act she also revealed how Alice Knowles had stayed at her house the night before her death. She had told her she was afraid to go home but had given no reason. After returning to her home the following morning, while her husband was at work, she had returned to Mrs. Windle's in the afternoon. It became apparent as the proceedings developed that Mrs. Windle and Alice Knowles had sent the youngsters out to bring them jugs of ale at frequent intervals during the afternoon and evening of the tragic day.

The prosecution pressed for a charge of Wilful Murder to be placed against Robert Knowles, stating that he had committed an unlawful act and was responsible for the consequences. When the defence Counsel gave a reply their message was that Knowles had been subjected to great hardship by his wife's conduct. Did anyone believe that when he struck her a blow he had any intention of killing her? If not then the case was one of manslaughter and not murder.

When the Coroner addressed the Inquest Jury, he told them to be guided solely by the evidence and not by what the advocates had said. To his mind the evidence pointed to a case of Manslaughter rather than Wilful Murder although that would be for the Jury to decide.

The Jury had a short deliberation and when they returned into court they brought a verdict of 'Manslaughter' against Robert Knowles. He was subsequently committed for trial at the forthcoming Manchester Assizes.

On the last Friday in November, 1888, the Preston tragedy was relived again in Manchester Crown Court before Mr. Justice Grantham. On being called, the prisoner walked up to the front of the dock, and in answer to the indictment said in a firm voice, "Not Guilty." He appeared deeply dejected, but it was manifest that he laboured under considerable emotion, which he made a determined effort to suppress. Eventually, however, his pent-up emotions broke out and he sobbed bitterly.

It was stressed from the start that Knowles was an industrious man and that, except when his wife gave way to drink, they had lived together comfortably. It was thought necessary to call the prisoner's eight-year-old daughter to give evidence and she very bravely and intelligently gave her version of the tragedy. She stated that when her mother fell from the chair, her father had pushed his foot by the side of her face. Very carefully she also gave an account of the fact that she had been sent during the course of the day for two half gallons and six gills of ale which were all consumed by her mother and Mrs. Windle.

The Defence Counsel stressed very much the behaviour that day of the two women who had spent their time 'boozing', while a little child went without food. Indeed, he suggested , would it not be more appropriate for Ellen Windle to be standing in the dock rather than the poor man before them.

When Mr. Justice Grantham summed up, he told the Jury that he did not see how they could come to any other conclusion except that the woman died from the result of the blow.

After five minutes consideration the Jury returned a verdict of 'Guilty' with a strong recommendation to mercy. At this point the Chief Constable of Preston, Major Little, was allowed to speak and he gave the prisoner a good character reference. His Lordship in passing sentence, said that it was a very sad case and he quite sympathised

Major Francis Little (pictured with the Earl Street Police Station in the background) spoke on behalf of the prisoner

with the Jury in the view they had taken of it. This was a serious matter. The prisoner had kicked the woman with his clogs, he had kicked her when she was down and helpless. It was a warning to other people of the great danger that was likely to result from the use of the clog, which was far too frequent in that part of the country. It was cowardly for a man to use his clogs, especially on a woman. However, he was in this case pleased to act on the Jury's recommendation of mercy and would pass a very lenient sentence. The sentence being that Robert Knowles be imprisoned for one calendar month with hard labour.

Preston's Nineteenth-century Chief Constables

PRESTON BOROUGH POLICE

PRESTON Borough Police was established under a Corporation Act of 1815, some thirteen years prior to the forming of the Metropolitan Police. Preston's first Chief Constable was Thomas Walton, who originally worked as a reed maker. Under his command he had one inspector and five ordinary constables. His annual salary amounted to about £250 which included a shilling for every summons issued; 3 shillings and six pence for every warrant executed; and twenty shillings for each deserter apprehended within the Borough.

In 1832, when John Addison was appointed Mayor, he presented the Police of the Borough with their first official suits. The uniform was deemed so precious that it was worn on Sundays only.

Under Mr. Walton's guidance the force, though small, was efficient and disciplined and he gave the Borough ardent, faithful and untiring service. In all he remained head of the Preston Borough Police for twenty-one years.

He was succeeded by Mr. Samuel Bannister who was to lead the Police through seventeen turbulent years. During a period marked by election and cotton riots he was instrumental in increasing the strength of the constabulary. In 1850 the force was fifteen strong, three for day duty and the remainder on night patrol. One year later Mr. Bannister had 28 officers under his control, as the value of an efficient body to preserve order began to be appreciated.

After Mr. Bannister's retirement in 1853, the force was handed to the care of Mr. Joseph Gibbons during whose time the new police station in Earl Street was opened. Just prior to that the Lancashire County Constabulary came to town with their first headquarters in Grimshaw Street.

Mr. Gibbons was Chief Constable for ten years, covering the time of great poverty due to the 'cotton famine' when the famished inhabitants had to be treated with understanding.

In 1863, after Mr. Gibbons' resignation, there were 140 applications for the position of Chief Constable, and the person selected was the Superintendent of Police for Swansea, Mr. James Dunn. The new Chief Constable had a family of eight children, but all save two sons had died at Swansea.

His years in charge were testing ones, particularly for the recently formed plain clothes branch. In addition to the usual criminal activities they had, on average, a couple of murders a year to attend to.

Gradually the size of the force was increasing and the Annual Report of 1871 showed 88 men in the Borough force, with a further 14 vacancies. The total cost of the Borough Police that year was just over £6,000.

Chief Constable Dunn did, during his time, have certain disagreements with the local Councillors, and there was also a lack of co-operation between the County and Borough Forces. All the differences of opinion though paled into insignificance in 1872, when Mr. Dunn's health dramatically declined. After a short illness he died, aged only 48, at his residence, 15 Stephenson Terrace, bringing an abrupt end to his nine years in charge.

The next appointment to Chief Constable was made from within, with Mr. Joseph Oglethorpe being raised to the post. He had been in the force some years and risen through the ranks. He became a popular leader and took in his stride all the labour riot troubles, the increasing number of fires and the usual mixture of serious and petty crime. In Guild Year 1882, Mr. Oglethorpe retired with a pension and he received a gold watch and chain from the members of an appreciative police force.

He was succeeded by Preston's first military Chief Constable Major F.L.G. Little. He had, since 1878, been the Superintendent of the Altrincham division of the Cheshire Constabulary. Prior to that he had enjoyed a distinguished military career. In 1861, aged 20, he had, whilst serving in Honduras, been appointed to command an expeditionary force of the Royal Artillery. Then came a spell as Fort Lieutenant to the Governor of Jersey and a couple of years as District Adjutant in the Isle of Wight. The last five years of his military service, which ended in 1878, were spent as Adjutant and Paymaster of the Royal Glamorgan Artillery Militia.

The new Chief Constable of Preston was soon embroiled in the task of controlling a force that had risen to almost one hundred men and cost close to £9,000 per annum to run. His salary of £350 per annum was reward for long hours spent supervising a Borough where crime was at worrying levels.

The detection rate was good although there were, inevitably, those who escaped the administers of justice. Major Little took a deep interest in the cases that attracted high public curiosity and on a number of occasions pleaded on behalf of the accused at their criminal trials.

Gradually Major Little was able to prove through the statistical returns that the Borough of Preston was becoming a safer haven in which to reside. In fact, in his eighteenth Annual Report – the last one of the nineteenth century – he was able to state that for the year ending the 31st December 1899, there had been a material decrease in all manner of offences. The total number of indictable offences being 188 as against 239 in the preceding year.

Not only did Major Francis Little take Preston's police force into the 20th century, but he remained in control until 1908, when Lionel D.L. Everett became Chief Constable. Major Little, who was born in 1841 died in 1914. In his latter days he became somewhat of a character and many old Prestonians later told amusing stories of 'T'owd Major'.

NINETEENTH-CENTURY CHIEF CONSTABLES OF PRESTON

Thomas Walton	1815 - 1836
Samuel Bannister	1836 - 1853
Joseph Gibbons	1853 - 1863
James Dunn	1863 - 1872
Joseph Oglethorpe	1872 - 1882
Francis Little	1882 - 1908

AMIDST THE FAMISHED PRESTON POOR

THE most serious and extensive season of distress through which Preston has ever passed was that caused by the 'cotton famine', which set in towards the end of 1861 and continued until almost the middle of 1865. This never-to-be-forgotten event was not owing to any renewed dispute between masters and men, but was a result of that desolating and memorable civil war in America, which prevented the raw material from being imported from the United States. This dearth of cotton was the harbinger of liberty to the slaves in the United States of America.

The cotton trade of Lancashire was paralysed as a black cloud suddenly burst upon our people and smashed their hopes. The great chimneys ceased to smoke, the whirling machinery was brought to a standstill and the spindles and looms became as hushed as if it was eternal night.

As a result poverty reigned supreme amongst the operatives and by the winter of 1862 the full effect of the 'cotton famine' was being felt. Winter and poverty are two severe tests which none but the poor properly understand. Singularly they may be confronted with fortitude and borne with patience; but when combined they constitute a terrible crucible which even the most enduring shrink from, and which none can pass through without pain, trouble and sorrow.

To the operatives of Preston the double source of suffering had become an unparalleled fact – a reality inflexible in its nature, and full of the bitterest privations in its effect. In an effort to assess the situation a number of directors of the Relief Fund made a visit to homes in the St. George's ward of the town. Those visited were typical of a cross-section of families struggling to come to terms with their dire situation.

The first visit was to the home of an out-of-work gardener in Hope Street. He had six children who, before the crisis came, had been working in a factory. The family's total earnings in the good times had been about £2 per week. There were now however four of them on the parish, receiving 2 shillings each per week and a younger daughter still working and earning 3s.6d. In all, the household of eight had a total income of 11s.6d per week which, according to the mother, was all they had to pay rent, fire, food and everything else.

The house had evidently been, in good times, a paragon of a place. The furniture, though sparse was neat and clean; the walls, though rather bare of pictures, were well swept and the floor, not carpeted or hearth rugged, was equally clean. There was, in the appearance of both the room and the residents, everything to bespeak that this was, before the hard times came, a happy home. They had been off work, or working very short time, for fourteen months and for a long period had preferred to eke out their savings as a supplement to the pittance the children earned, rather than be at the mercy of official charity. Only when their savings had been expended had they applied for relief and even that 'evil day' had been averted by the pledging of some of their clothes. The mother telling her visitors, "If I had as much clothing again, I would pawn it rather than go on the parish. I'd try to keep above the rest as long as I'd a stitch about me that I could spare. I've been a thinking and hoping that times would mend; but at last we were like to go to the parish." The next home visited was in Back Canal Street, where the unemployed father had a wife, five children and an adopted child to take care of. The house had been dependent on factory earnings and four of the children were capable of working, with the income in prosperous times amounting to 34 shillings per week. Alas! There was now no work for them to do and they needed recourse to other means of obtaining a subsistence. One had been out of work seven months, another thirteen months and all they could scrape together, including the allowance from the parish and the charitable fund, did not amount to more than 10s.6d per week. They too had been thrifty souls but now their clothing had nearly all gone, and bedding too, and all for food.

The shirts of the lads were complete pieces of patchwork, through dint of constant mending; the woman's bed gown stitched and 'fettled', as it had often been, was a marvel in how it was holding together. The frock of the poor creature reminded the visitors of Joseph's coat of many colours, so often had it undergone repair. The bed clothes they had left were not quite so bad as the wearing apparel; but they had not sufficient of them to keep them warm a-nights and had to make shift with what tackle they had.

A couple of doors further along the street the inmates were in a similar forlorn condition. The man was a spinner and he had a wife and two children. For fifteen months he had been out of work and had been struggling ever since to get a crust for his dependants. Not one of them had a stocking on their feet and they were rejoicing because a ragged old coat, which in ordinary times their pride would have scorned, had been given to one of the lads by a kind benefactor. So bad was the condition of this family that they had to sit naked whilst their tattered under-linen was being washed.

While still in Back Canal Street the visitors called at the house of a steam loom weaver, his wife and eight children. They could, when in full work, bring in 35 shillings per week, but come the hard times they were surviving on 14 shillings per week. Some of them had not worked for the last thirteen months and to get food their clothing had also been sold, or pledged. All they had in the way of apparel was to be seen on their backs, and they too, in order to cleanliness, had to adopt the expedient resorted to by the inmates of the previous house. One of the lads was more decently attired than the rest, having on a good substantial fustian jacket and a pair of trousers. They had been given to him by a good samaritan belonging to the Orchard School. Sadly, those clothes were about to be pledged in order to get food or a 'bit of firing'.

The next visit was to Back Hope Street, the house of an Irish family of seven persons. For fourteen weeks there had never been a fire in the grate. Amongst them were three young teenage women, and they crouched with shame behind each other because of their comparative nakedness. They possessed no clothing save what they had on, and they too had to wash their apparel by night. As badly off, if not worse, were they for bedding. Upstairs was a rickety old bedstead, which, if offered for sale on the Orchard, would not have fetched 6d. The cords were all broken and on these was a cotton tick, out of which fell the chaff with which it had been filled. Of bed-clothes, there was actually none, and there in this small, badly ventilated chamber, lay a-nights the whole family. James, with his father and mother on the bed, the littlest boy at the foot, and the three young women huddled together on the floor. They had possessed another pair of bedsteads, but had been obliged to sell them for 2s.6d. with which they had bought some food, after they had been without for two days.

At another house lived a grinder, who, when times were good, with the joint earnings of his wife, got 24 shillings per week. They had five children but all that was available for their support was 9 shillings per week. That day all this honest worker had eaten was a small portion of the soup that had been dispensed from the soup kitchen.

In Savage's Court, lying on a thing not worthy of the name of a bed, a poor woman in an apparently hopeless and dying condition. Her poor attenuated arms bespoke what she must have suffered and her hoarse voice told of the approaching departure from a world of woe. She had been sick a year and there she lay actually coverless and almost clothesless, crouching in the hope of retaining her inner heat. Her husband had some months before been lying by her side but sickness had consumed him and he had passed away. There were three little children, all in rags and squalor, about the bedside and they were crying for something to eat.

Next, to the house of a factory worker, whose wife and five children were starving for want of fire, but coals they had none, nor fuel. The husband was away serving 21 days in gaol for theft. His crime had been to take a couple of rails from a boarding on the railway near the Wellington Terrace to kindle a fire to warm his freezing family. Justice had been blind to the beseechings of mercy and while he served his sentence, his family was fatherless, fireless and foodless. When the Relief Committee had completed their tour of inspection they knew only too well the miseries that abounded. There was a great strain on the Poor Law Guardians and they had to relieve thousands of people.

During the distress, the Guardians employed the able-bodied males, who were receiving relief, on various tasks. There was stone braking at a yard off Leighton Street; earth excavating and levelling at the Cattle Market; on the Moor; and at the Union Workhouse in Fulwood.

The management of these enterprises and the distribution of relief was not without its problems and trouble arrived in April, 1863. For some months the men labouring at the Cattle Market and on the Moor had, through deficiency of working plant, been employed only half the time named in their orders, but had been paid as if they had worked the whole of it. When a sufficient supply of plant was obtained, the Guardians resolved that the men should return to working full time, with the pay remaining unchanged, at one shilling and a small bag of meal for each day.

This action on the part of the Guardians was keenly opposed by the men who went on strike. Then some of the men returned to the places where they had been working and idled away their time, under the impression that appearance only was required to ensure payment. They were of course told that this sort of thing would not do, and if they did not work, they would not be paid.

Deductions were made in proportion to the non-compliance of the men and much dissatisfaction was caused. The whole situation coming to a head on Tuesday, April 20th, 1863.

A notice had been posted warning of the intention to deduct pay and a number set about their tasks with enthusiasm, but others lounged around all day. That afternoon rain fell and the work was stopped with the men going to the Workhouse where, at five o'clock, they would receive their daily payment. When they presented themselves, however, the labour-masters and timekeepers pointed out those who had been larking around.

The officials had been given strict instructions and many were only offered six pence for their day's work. The men declared that they had not eaten for a considerable length of time, and that their wives and families were awaiting their arrival to obtain the means of procuring a meal. Some of the men said they would take their children to the Union Offices in Lancaster Road and leave them either to die or be taken in by the officials there.

Eventually the men left the Workhouse in a body and proceeded into the town. They made their way in procession through the streets to the police station, where, it was understood, the Mayor, Mr. Philip Park, and Mr. Ascroft (the chairman of the Board of Guardians) were conferring together.

The famished mob besieged the police station and loud cries went up for 'Mr. Livesey' – who ultimately appeared and addressed them

They arrived at the police station a little after six o'clock, and it was suggested that a deputation should meet the Mayor, Mr. Park and Mr. Ascroft to explain their grievances. Six of their body were invited into the Mayor's Parlour and Mr. Joseph Livesey was also asked to attend, to assist them in coming to an amicable settlement. During the consultation the crowd, which had increased considerably to upwards of 8,000 persons, began to become very impatient, crying out for the deputation to be sent out.

After a lengthy conference the deputation appeared and one of their number ascended a windowsill and addressed the multitude. He told them that those who had worked the proper time and had been booked, would be paid, and that those who had gone away or had neglected their work, would not be paid. All, he said, would be remedied on the following day.

Strong protestations were made against the decision which had been arrived at. The people shouted out that they were hungering and that they and their children must have food, whatever decision was come to. Soon after this a great effort was made by the crowd to get into the police station, but they were prevented by the police and order was maintained.

At this point there were loud cries for "Mr. Livesey" who ultimately appeared and addressed the assemblage. He impressed upon them the desirability of keeping the peace and advised them to go home quietly. The crowd were, however, restless and becoming excitable, they began to hurl brickbats and stones at the constables who defended the station doorway.

After this had been carrying on some time, a body of police, with their truncheons and under the command of Superintendent Dunn, made a charge upon the mob and succeeded in clearing the Orchard in a few minutes, as the crowd ran off in all directions. Superintendent Dunn was hit in several places, but not seriously and a number of constables were injured in the manoeuvre. One officer was hit on the cheek with a paving stone, a couple were hit on the forehead and others received facial cuts and bruises, arm and leg injuries. The sufferers were conveyed back into the police station where their wounds were dressed by a medical man.

A number of the mob were arrested for riotous behaviour and the Mayor left the police station in a cab, bound for the Fulwood Barracks. At ten minutes past nine he arrived back in town, along with 250 foot soldiers, under military command. The disturbance

Preston's Police station in Earl Street had to be guarded by the military as the hungry mob marched into town

had, however, been subdued by the Borough Police before the soldiers arrived and their services were not required.

After discussions with the police, half the military men returned to the Barracks and the remainder took up position in the Orchard, in front of the police station. They remained there until ten o'clock when orders were issued for them to also depart and return to the Barracks.

The disturbance was not renewed after the soldiers left and rumours of attacks on individual's homes proved unfounded and all was quiet throughout the night.

The following morning three youths, Richard Pye, joiner, William Harrison, creeler and James Hoyle, joiner were brought up at the Police Court. They were charged with throwing stones and committing a riot on the previous evening. A number of constables gave evidence against the threesome and they were committed for trial.

Whilst the magisterial inquiry was being conducted, the parish labourers were parading the streets. All the men had met in the morning at the usual time, on the Moor and at the Cattle Market. Still in an agitated state they resolved to throw down their tools and a handful who were reluctant to take part in any further disturbance, were stoned by some youths.

The general body then walked in processional order to the town. They marched through the Orchard, down Orchard Street and Friargate and along Lune Street to the Corn Exchange. It was generally known that the Guardians held a school for unemployed youths at the Exchange, and the mob attacked the building. The doors were kicked, two or three panes of glass were broken and in length of time the men succeeded in bringing the scholars out of the place and into the street.

The crowd then proceeded to Winckley Square and the residence of Mr. Park, the Mayor. When they enquired if his Worship was within they received a reply in the negative. After knocking at the doors of a couple of other prominent citizens and receiving similar negative responses, the mob resolved to return to the Orchard.

The famished rioters kicked the doors of the Corn Exchange, and shattered panes of glass as they demanded the scholars inside join their procession of protest

There, they held a meeting using an empty cart as a rostrum for the speakers. Several men mounted the cart and addressed the multitude, although much of their speech was drowned by a section of noisy and turbulent youths. There was talk of another deputation being sent to the Mayor.

Suddenly though, a cry was raised, "The soldiers are coming," and this had the effect of dispersing the meeting. The sight of three divisions of infantry from Fulwood Barracks, with fixed bayonets marching along Lancaster Road, was enough to send the mob scurrying up the Orchard.

The soldiers took up their position immediately in front of the police station and formed a guard. Their appearance had created great excitement and a vast crowd collected around them.

The time was fast approaching mid-day and in one of the rooms of the police station were the Mayor, the Town Clerk and several Magistrates. They soon received a message stating that the men in the Orchard wanted to have an interview. The Mayor was, in view of the previous evening's turbulent proceedings, reluctant to grant their wish. As a result, Superintendent Dunn summoned all his officers and the members of the fire brigade and gave the crowd to understand that they had better disperse, warning them that if they persisted then the Mayor would read the Riot Act and that they then would have to take the consequences.

The police and the fire brigade at once turned out of the building and began to clear the crowd. They spread themselves in all directions and soon drove the multitude of persons before them. A few seemed determined to maintain their ground; but the police sharply made them budge and in a few minutes the main part of the Orchard was cleared. The general bulk of the parish labourers behaved themselves well and showed no resistance to the police. Indeed, those most difficult to deal with were the noisy females and rough youths.

After being removed from the square, the people took up their position on the northern side of the road which ran in front of the Methodist Chapel. The police, however, wanted them further removed and a little persuasion led to them dispersing in various directions, some going along Lancaster Road, others up High Street and Back Lane and many down Orchard Street and into Friargate.

Within minutes information was received at the police station that some of the men had commenced begging in the streets in gangs. They were calling at shops and asking for provisions and stopping people in the street and asking for money. Nervous people imagined that this was the prelude to a kind of bread riot and the next step would be an attack upon the provisions shops.

Fortunately, when the police officers threatened those who were begging with arrest, they gave over. In the next couple of hours a number of minor incidents occurred but generally the parish labourers were keen to return to work. The men who worked at the Moor were in general back at work by two o'clock. At the Cattle Market the men, although intimating their willingness to work, could not get their tools because they were locked in a storeroom. A few of the rougher element began throwing stones about and a policeman was struck by one of the missiles. Fortunately he was not much hurt. Nonetheless, a rumour soon reached town that the men were fighting furiously and officers were in danger of being killed.

Consequently the Mayor hurried to the place with a body of the military. The services of the military were not required and the Mayor went amongst the men to discuss their difficulties. There was still discontent over the money the men were to receive. Eventually, at six o'clock that evening, the Mayor returned to the police station. He informed all that there had been no row on the cattle market, that the men had generally 'fallen in' concerning the acceptance of pay and that generally the town was cooling down.

That evening there was little trouble save for some stone throwing and regular dispersing of any large numbers who gathered in the vicinity of the Orchard. The military were ordered back to their quarters and by midnight all was tranquil.

At the proper hour on the Thursday morning the whole of the men resumed their work and generally kept to it most assiduously. Their action had been helped by an official plea, from the Cotton Spinners Association, calling for their members to keep the peace.

In the middle of May at the Preston Intermediate Sessions the trial of the Preston rioters took place before Mr. Thomas Batty Addison. Besides the three charged with unlawful assembly on the Tuesday, a further five were placed on trial for disturbing the peace the following day. They were Owen Clarke, aged 22, Michael McGough, aged 18, John Hartley, aged 18, James Wilcock, aged 24 and Jeremiah Cohen who was 19 years old.

When the cases of the first three were considered, William Harrison pleaded Guilty and both James Hoyle and Richard Pye were found Guilty after a short deliberation by the Jury. The second group were mainly concerned with stone throwing, which caused considerable damage to an office in the stone-yard, Leighton Street. A couple of the labour masters identified the accused men as being amongst the hundred or so gathered at that place in a riotous manner. After a short deliberation, all five accused were found guilty of riotous behaviour.

At this point, all the eight prisoners were placed in the dock and the learned Chairman told them they were a disgrace to the town, whose people for so many months had behaved so well during distress. The operatives hitherto had, by their conduct, earned the praise of the whole world for the patient suffering they had shown.

The Chairman then informed the culprits of their sentences, with Richard Pye, James Hoyle, William Harrison, Owen Clarke and John Hartley receiving a six month's prison term and Michael McGough and James Wilcock, who were regarded as ringleaders in the riot, being sentenced to twelve month's imprisonment. Finally Jeremiah Cohen, who had been in prison at least six times previously, was informed that he was sentenced to three years penal servitude.

The events of the week in April, 1863 had highlighted the acute problems facing the cotton operatives of the town and it was to be two more years before some normality returned to the life of the Borough's inhabitants. The Preston Relief Committee had begun their work in January, 1862 and they continued it with much vigour and regularity until the middle of May, 1865. In all, the Committee spent the sum of £131,000 in relief of the local district. The Relief Committee had spent the main portion of their funds on food, including 1,298,288 sixpenny loaves and the distribution of over one million sixpenny tickets, which enabled the distressed to purchase food from the town's provision shops. The Committee utilised a large empty mill off Lancaster Road, in Crooked Lane, as their central store. During the distress a long line of men, women and children could often be seen standing patiently by the side of the place, with jugs, cans and bowls in their hands, ready to be served, in turn, with soup and such other food as might be deemed necessary. The greatest number of persons relieved by the Committee was in December, 1862 when 40,627 received the life-saving aid.

The Relief Committee, God bless them! They gave food to the hungry, clothes to the naked and coals for the fireless grates. Out of all the suffering and poverty the town's people emerged with pride.

As the distress continued, long lines of men, women, and children waited with patience to be served soup. The scene was typical throughout Lancashire – Preston folk queued in Crooked Lane off Lancaster Road.

Verse to Preston Poor

If proof you seek of what I say
    Walk by the Preston Moor,
And there, at work, or else at play,
    You'll find the Preston poor.

To aid the well-deserving man,
    And those who worthy seem,
There lives and works a glorious plan —
    The Bedding Charity Scheme.

Those in this scheme, who take the lead,
    Could many a tale unfold,
Of hearts made glad in time of need,
    And still the tale's untold;

For many more, aye, many a score,
    In vain implore relief.
May timely aid soon reach their door,
    To soothe them in their grief.

I dearly wish, throughout the land,
    We more would love each other;
And, though one's poor, stretch out our hand,
    And call him still a brother.

For surely in this blessed clime,
    Though threatened by the Gaul,
We each should join the merry chime —
    "There's room enough for all."

AFTER MIDNIGHT ON STONE BRIDGE BROW

IN the middle of the last week in May, 1863 John Jackson, a boiler maker of Preston journeyed to Lancaster with a boiler, which needed some specialist work doing to it in that place. Mr. Jackson gave the contract for transportation to John and Thomas Slater, who agreed to convey it on a lorry pulled by six horses, five of which the Slaters supplied.

Aware of the enormity of the task, the Slaters also recruited two other carters from Lancaster, namely John Parkinson and James Simpson and the four contractors, along with Mr. Jackson, set off on their trek. The journey to Lancaster was a slow and cautious one, which the boiler maker's party negotiated successfully.

The necessary work was duly carried out and by Friday evening the boiler was ready for its return trip. Responsibility for particular horses was given to each of the five men, and the boiler was the responsibility of all.

The haulage work on a summer's evening soon built up a thirst and when they got to the top of Penny Street in Lancaster the men had a quart of beer amongst them. The next stop on their journey was Scotforth and at that place, along with four or five other men, they consumed half a gallon of ale.

By the time they got to Galgate, the horses needed watering, and while the animals quenched their thirsts, the men did also with a pint of beer apiece. A further stop followed at Old Hollins, and there the hauliers had another glass of ale each. This sustained the men until they reached Garstang, at which point they ordered something to eat and washed it down with another half gallon of beer.

From Garstang to Myerscough the men took careful charge of the horses and sluggish, but safe, progress was made. At Myerscough the two Slaters, being somewhat more tired than the others, requested that they be allowed to get into the boiler to have a sleep. It was understood that they would be awakened when they had got as far as Stone Bridge Brow, in Barton – a very steep hill declining towards

Preston. It was the duty of one of the Slaters to look after the wheel-lock and his services would be particularly required for descending the hill.

The horses, with Mr. Jackson in charge of the shaft horse, moved along the road at an average speed. Some of them were thought of as rather spirited, but none were considered to be of the unmanageable class.

Shortly after midnight the party reached the top of Stone Bridge Brow. Mr. Jackson gave the requisite signal and the horses and lorry were stopped. He and John Parkinson, who had charge of the next horse, then walked towards the rear of the boiler with a view to waking the Slaters, in order that one of them might put on the lock, whilst the other took charge of a fore horse.

No sooner, however, had Jackson and Parkinson left their horses than one of the animals gave a 'twitch' forward. This act set the whole of the horses in motion, and they pulled the lorry over the edge of the brow. Jackson ran to the shaft horse and tried to stop it, but unable to do so he shouted out, "We are done."

Despite Parkinson attempting to stop his horse the whole proceeded down the hill. In order to keep the horses in a line and prevent the waggon from overtaking them, Parkinson used his whip and got the horses in a kind of gallop. Through this he kept them well ahead; but when they were within twenty yards of the bottom of the hill three of the horses fell and were killed.

As soon as the animals had fallen, and when the waggon had partially run over them, Parkinson looked round for Jackson. He could not see him anywhere and fearing that something had happened, he turned back to look for him.

He did not have to go very far before he found Jackson lying in the ditch side, about twenty yards from the top of the hill, and quite dead. He had evidently been run over for there was a wheel mark right up one of his arms to the shoulder.

The other men were all safe. The Slaters having remained in the boiler until the waggon came to a standstill. Assistance was at once procured and the body of John Jackson was removed to the Shuttleworth's Arms, in Broughton.

Later that Saturday morning the horses were taken out of their harnesses and despatched in the ordinary manner.

The same evening the inquest was opened before Mr. Miles Myers into the untimely death of the 45-year-old boiler maker. After

The body of the unfortunate John Jackson was removed to the Shuttleworth Arms at Broughton

formal identification, it was then adjourned until the following Wednesday.

On that day the fatal journey was recalled and witnesses were questioned on the state of the men considering the amount of alcoholic refreshment they had taken. One of them, a provisions dealer from Catterall said, "I can't say that they were perfectly sober, or that they were drunk."

Whatever their state of intoxication, it had been a shocking incident and the Inquest Jury returned with the verdict 'Accidentally killed.'

WIFE KILLING IN GARDNER STREET

AMONG the residents of Gardner Street, off North Road, in December, 1868, were the Caton family. Both Robert Caton, aged 45 and his wife Ann, aged 43, had been married before and they shared their home with their two grown-up children from previous marriages. Robert Caton having a 16-year-old daughter called Ellen, who worked as a power loom weaver, and Ann Caton having a son named Henry Ogle.

The Caton marriage was a far from harmonious one with both Robert Caton, who worked as a plasterer and whitewasher and his wife Ann being given to drink. For some time the husband had been in the habit of buying-in all provisions and necessities for the house, as when the money was given to his wife she invariably spent it on liquor. This fact angered Ann Caton very much and as the daughter seemed to enjoy more of her husband's confidence than she did, she grew very jealous of her.

Fights between the married couple were of frequent occurrence and regarded as commonplace by the neighbouring residents. When Ann Caton could not get money from her husband for drink she was often seen visiting the pawnshop with household articles.

On Saturday, 5th December, 1868, some time after seven o'clock, Robert Caton visited a provision shop in North Road, along with his daughter Ellen for the purpose of buying some provisions. They had been in the shop only a short time when Ann Caton arrived on the premises. She appeared to be somewhat intoxicated and began cursing and swearing. Her husband and his daughter were called all sorts of opprobrious names and eventually the shop proprietor ordered Mrs. Caton's departure. In no fit state to be reasoned with she returned within a couple of minutes, threatening to smash the shop window if not readmitted. Robert Caton was by now incensed by his wife's behaviour and raising his hand he struck her on the mouth.

Ann Caton at once left the shop, stating she was going for a policeman, but in fact got no further than the vault of the nearby Royal George beerhouse. There she drank a couple of beers and after conversing with a neighbouring couple from Gardner Street, she returned home.

Meanwhile Robert Caton, who also stated he was going in search of a policeman when he left the shop, returned home briefly and then at the daughter's insistence, went with her to buy a shawl. They visited a pawnshop in the High Street and another in Lancaster Road, but as the daughter was unable to see one which suited her, they returned home empty-handed.

With husband and wife once again at their Gardner Street home their abusive conversation was recommenced. Ann Caton accused her husband of, amongst other things, living tally with his own daughter and the latter of having a child by him.

The woman who seemed too drunk to stand, then lay down on the sofa while an enraged Robert Caton disappeared into the cellar. When he returned into the living room he had in his hand a stick and, approaching his wife, he struck her three violent blows on the head and arm.

When he had done this she said to him, "You had better do it again", and he responded by hitting her three more times in the same places. At this point his daughter Ellen interfered between the pair and persuaded her father to leave off striking his wife.

The daughter then asked her father to go again with her to find a shawl and Ann Caton was left alone in the house, in a drunken state and groaning from the beating inflicted upon her. This time the daughter's search for a shawl was successful, with her father purchasing it for her from a shop in Kilshaw Street. He then told his daughter he was going to visit the Iron Duke beerhouse in North Road and she returned home. As the daughter approached the house she was met by James Edward Ainsworth, a young man with whom she had been keeping company. Once inside the house they observed Mrs. Caton still laid on the sofa moaning and groaning with a shawl partly covering her head and face. For another two hours she was left in that state while Ellen Caton entertained her boyfriend. It was only when Mrs. Caton's son arrived home that she was given any further attention and when he removed the shawl that partly covered her face he realised that she was dead. He at once raised the alarm and Ellen Caton, along with her boyfriend, went to the Iron Duke beerhouse to relay the news to Robert Caton.

A police constable was soon on the scene and when Caton returned home the officer apprehended him. He looked at his wife and said, "She is dead." He then went to the cellar and brought out the stick with which he had committed the fatal deed and giving it to the constable said, "I struck her three times with that." Caton, who was by now much more intoxicated than when he committed the act, was taken to the police station and charged with the 'Wilful Murder' of his wife.

On the Sunday, the scene of the tragedy was visited by large numbers and the smallest item of news in regard to the murder was eagerly seized and commented upon. Rumours were current that while in the Iron Duke he had used the following phrases: "I have just left Ann taking her last sleep" and "I have done for her now." The landlord however, insisted that Robert Caton had acted in his usual manner, being quite calm and collected when he arrived and quietly drinking his glasses of ale.

The inquest on the death of Ann Caton was held on the Monday afternoon at the police court, before Miles Myres, Esq. the Coroner. The tragic events were relived and a local surgeon reported on his attendance upon the dead woman and the subsequent post-mortem.

The skull had been battered in a most horrible manner and the only wonder was that the unfortunate woman survived for over two hours after receiving the fatal blows. The fractures were caused by very severe blows and the murder weapon, which was half of a broom handle, must have been used with great force. The inquest jury decided that Robert Caton should be committed for trial on a charge of manslaughter. The following afternoon, when the Magistrates made a further examination of the prisoner and the evidence available they decided he should stand trial on the more serious charge of 'Wilful Murder'. The prisoner who throughout the hearing had preserved the utmost coolness, was then committed to take his trial at the next Lancaster Assizes.

On the first Thursday in March, 1869 he appeared before Mr. Justice Lush and the Grand Jury, whose foreman was Robert Townley Parker, the Preston Guild Mayor of 1862. By the time Robert Caton stood in the Crown Court dock, the charge against him was reduced to one of 'Manslaughter' on the instructions of His Lordship. The trial was a short one, with Ellen Caton being called to once again outline the events of the night her stepmother died. When asked why she didn't attend to the groans of the injured woman, she said that she had done the same thing before when they had fallen out and she thought that she was pretending her husband had hurt her.

The Defence Counsel urged the Grand Jury to remember the great provocation that the prisoner had been forced to endure. His Lordship, in summing up the case, stated that no person could justify the taking away of the life of another person, except in self defence. There was no doubt, he continued, that the blows from the stick were the immediate cause of Ann Caton's death, hence the man was guilty of manslaughter.

After a short consultation, the Jury returned a verdict of 'Manslaughter under great provocation'. His Lordship then informed the court that he would need more time to consider the sentence.

Robert Townley Parker – the 1862 Guild Mayor was foreman of the Grand Jury that considered the case of Robert Caton accused of killing his third wife

Two days later Robert Caton was informed that, following the Jury's strong recommendation to mercy, he would be sentenced to twelve months' imprisonment, with hard labour.

AN ACT OF LUNACY AT THE ASYLUM

TOWARDS the end of March, 1878 a trial took place at Lancaster Assizes before Mr. Justice Lopes, in which John James Coupe, a lunatic asylum attendant at Whittingham Asylum, was indicted for inciting to murder.

The court was told that between Preston and Lancaster, on the Garstang side, there was a lunatic asylum, maintained at the expense of the county and within its boundaries were 1,200 lunatics.

The chain of events that had led to seventeen-year-old Coupe appearing in the dock had started on the 7th of January that year, when one of the cottages in which the warders slept was robbed. The cottages were situated in a block of twelve, about a quarter of a mile to the north of the main building.

Suspicion at first fell upon two warders called Kenyon and Bailey who slept in the cottages. However, these two men, upon an investigation, exculpated themselves and suspicion was transferred to Coupe. He was told not to sleep any more in the cottages, but to sleep in the main building and information was relayed to him that the Committee of Justices would meet at the asylum during the last week of January, when they would consider the charge against him made by Bailey, Kenyon and others.

At that time there was an inmate in the asylum named Jackson, who was a native of Australia and a seafaring man. He had been at Whittingham since the previous April, having been troubled with a sort of insanity or loss of mind. His stay in the asylum had appeared to benefit him and, having been a person of considerable intelligence, it was felt his release was imminent.

On the 12th of January, Coupe was seen in the company of Jackson and before they were interrupted, Coupe told the inmate that he had been the subject of persecution by Kenyon and Bailey and that if Jackson would rob their cottage a £20 reward would be his. Exactly a week later Coupe proposed that Jackson carry out his plans which by this time included the murder of the wardens Kenyon and Bailey. Coupe outlined his scheme to the inmate who outwardly appeared to accept the proposals.

Whittingham Asylum formally opened in 1873 – five years later an Asylum attendant was accused of inciting to murder

Jackson's instructions were that at half past four on the following Monday evening, he should first of all rob the cottage in which warder Kenyon slept and murder him with a long sharp instrument. The instrument and a chisel to break open the cash boxes, being provided for him by Coupe.

Having killed Kenyon, he was then to go to the cottage where Bailey slept and provide himself with clothing, with which to make good his escape.

After he had committed that crime his instructions were to meet Coupe at the rustic bridge, which passed over a culvert or stream some 300 yards to the south of the main asylum building. Once there the pair of them would wait for the arrival of Bailey who, every Monday afternoon, journeyed into Preston for various articles.

Punctuality was apparently one of his virtues because he always arrived at the rustic bridge at a quarter to six o'clock in the evening. As Bailey drove up Jackson was to ask him for a lift back to the asylum. Then, on getting into the cart, he was to run Bailey through with the same instrument, throw Bailey over the bridge and the horse's head was to be turned towards Preston.

Jackson was then to change into the clothes he had stolen and accompanied by Coupe, the pair were to cross the fields to Preston, where he would be placed on a train bound for London. Coupe stating that he would then return to the asylum without his absence being noticed.

When Jackson got to London he was to write to Coupe, who had provided him with this address: Cow Hill, Fulwood, near Preston, Lancashire, England.

At that time each warder in the asylum was furnished with keys, some of which unlocked the cottages. At night, the asylum doors were double locked and there was a strict rule that none of the warders should part with his keys. Coupe showed the seriousness of his intention by handing over his keys to the inmate Jackson.

As things transpired Jackson had enough about him to realise the lunacy of Coupe's suggestions and the next day he told his tale to a man called Bateman, who in turn communicated with the asylum authorities, including Dr. Holland.

The doctor, on hearing the story, felt it was a most astounding thing and he himself questioned Jackson who was able to produce the sharp instrument, the chisel, the address written in Coupe's own handwriting and the keys.

Therefore, that Monday night Dr. Holland ordered several persons to station themselves close to the bridge where Coupe was to meet Jackson. Just before Bailey arrived, along came Coupe whistling merrily and, as he called out for Jackson, to his surprise there emerged from the bushes a number of persons who at once escorted him to the asylum.

It was apparent that had Jackson carried out the plot and got away, then it would have taken the suspicion of the other robbery away from Coupe and on to the shoulders of Jackson.

Once this tale had been outlined to the Jury at Lancaster Assizes and they had heard the testimony of Dr. Holland, and the inmate Jackson, it was left to Defence Counsel to attempt to discredit the case against Coupe.

Their suggestion was that while Coupe had incited Jackson to commit robbery he had not instructed him to murder and that the words of accusation had come from the mouth of a man confined for lunacy.

The Jury took little time over their deliberations and in less than ten minutes they had returned in court to delivery a Guilty verdict.

His Lordship in passing sentence told John James Coupe that he had been convicted on very clear evidence of a most audacious crime, the crime of inciting another to commit murder. He concluded by telling him that he was a person who ought to be removed from the community for as long as the law permits, and in consequence he handed the prisoner a term of ten years penal servitude.

Postscript:

Whittingham Asylum was formally opened on April Fools Day, 1873 and the weekly charge for the care of each pauper lunatic was 9s 11d per head for patients from within the county and 14s.0d for those who originated from other counties.

By the end of the first official year the patient population was over three hundred, comprising of roughly equal numbers of males and females.

Within five years, as the Asylum buildings increased, the number of inmates rose to 1,250 and a further five years on, as more annexes were added, 1,650 patients were in the care of the lunatic asylum authorities.

By the end of the nineteenth century the institution had additional hospital accommodation and the patient population had grown to over two thousand.

EDWARD LATHAM –
FOUND DEAD

O N Saturday, 29th September, 1849 the 'Preston Chroncle' carried the headline, 'Alleged Wilful Murder in Preston'. The article went on to inform the readers that considerable excitement had been occasioned in the town on Monday morning last, by the discovery of the body of 55-year-old Edward Latham, a former landlord of the Grey Horse public house who, at the time of his death, was employed as a gardener by Mrs. Pedder, of Ashton Lodge.

The body had been first discovered by Richard Hindle a local constable stationed at Ashton, who, proceeding under the arches of the Preston and Wyre Railway, at about 12.30am had spotted something lying in the highway. On going up to the place he had found Edward Latham lying on his back, quite dead. The spot was some thirty yards from the Rawstorne's Arms public house, at the bottom of Tulketh Brow.

The night was very light and there was no weapon or stick of any kind near to the deceased, who felt quite warm and had apparently not lain long. His hat was lying in the road, about eight or nine yards from the body, about such a distance as it might have been had the man fallen. The constable examined the body and there was a scar on the forehead and a mark on the thigh. Neither of them appeared to arise from blows, but as if from a fall. His clothes were not in a rough state, as if he had been ill treated; but were marked on one side as if he had fallen on that side.

As the constable attended to the man, a local shoemaker James Jolly, appeared on the scene and he helped the police officer to carry the body into the Rawstorne's Arms. A local surgeon was called to the public house and under the instructions of the Coroner Mr. Palmer, he made a post mortem examination of the body. He found several bruises upon the surface of the body and two small bruises upon the left side of the chest; a bruise, apparently an old one, on the left hip; another bruise on the left arm, just below the shoulder.

The left eye had received a slight cut, as if it had come in contact with a sharp stone. There was a bruise above the right eyelid, near the nose. The surgeon also discovered internal damage caused by the fracture of two ribs, which had led to laceration of the spleen and subsequent loss of blood. It was to this that the surgeon attributed the cause of death. He could not say positively what caused the fractures, but he felt that they may have risen from the deceased falling against the kerb stone of the footpath. Observing that if they had risen from a kick, or some other cause, the surface wound would have been much larger. He then suggested that the deceased may have arisen after the fracture of the ribs and have fallen again, on the greater effusion of blood taking place and this would have accounted for all the bruises on one side, which were not likely to have been produced from a single fall. Concerning the bruise on the nose and the marks upon the eyelids, he did not think that those could have been produced by a fall. He concluded by stating that with the exception of those marks he found nothing which seemed to have been occasioned by blows or violence inflicted by another person.

The inquest into Edward Latham's death was held on the Tuesday morning and besides the constable, and the surgeon who attended the deceased on the Monday morning, other witnesses were called to establish how he met his untimely end.

Alexander Giles, a local gardener, told the hearing that he had been with Latham from midday on the Sunday when they had dined together. Shortly after eleven o'clock that night the pair had entered the Watering Trough public

Edward Latham left the Watering Trough public house in Fylde Road around about midnight – later he was found dead

house in Fylde Road and, as they drank their glass of ale, they had become acquainted with a group of four other men. As they left the public house some time around midnight the other men, who were strangers to him, had set off down the road with them. He lived just a little further down than the public house and when he reached his home he shook hands with Latham, and Latham carried on down the road with the four other men. He stated that his friend had had a few glasses of ale but seemed perfectly capable of taking care of himself and could walk without stumbling, and that there was no quarrelling between Latham and any of the other men who accompanied him.

Henry Glover, a farm labourer from Lea, was next to be examined and he stated that he had called in at the Watering Trough to ask the landlord if any person there was going home his way. He was told that Edward Latham was, and when the deceased left the public house he accompanied him and the other men. By the time they had reached the Rawstorne's Arms at the bottom of the road, the other men had left them.

He then told the hearing that they knocked at the public house door but could not get in and realising he was not going to get any more to drink he left Latham knocking at the door and set off home. There were no other persons about when they parted and on the two and a half mile trek home he saw only one other person.

Elizabeth Eccles, the wife of the publican at the Rawstorne's Arms, recalled two men knocking at the door shortly after midnight on the night in question. She told them it was after filling time and sent them away. When they knocked again a second time a few minutes later she still refused to let them in. About half and hour afterwards Hindle, the policeman, knocked on the door and with the help of another man was carrying the deceased, who was quite dead. During the time before the constable arrived she heard no noise of quarrelling or fighting in the neighbourhood, nor anything which could arise from a person being abused or ill-treated.

After hearing the whole of the evidence the inquest jury retired to consider their verdict and when they returned they announced the following verdict – 'Found dead on the highway, having on his body several mortal fractures and bruises, but how or by what means those fractures were caused, no evidence appeared'.

The inconclusive outcome of the inquest left a great question mark over the whole affair. However, within a couple of days, fresh particulars emerged. A man named George Miller who resided at

Stock's Farm, in Ashton, heard about the melancholy occurrence that had taken place and knowing that one of his servants, a young man called Charles Billington, had been in the vicinity at the time enquired if he knew anything about it. On the day in question he had been, as his master knew, to Bamber Bridge and had returned home along the road on which the body was found.

At first he denied any knowledge of the affair, but with some embarrassment, and on Mr. Miller representing to him the responsibility which would attach to him if he knew anything of the occurrence and refused to satisfy the ends of justice, he burst into tears and at once confessed that he saw Glover ill-treating the deceased. His statement to Mr. Miller describing the following course of events:

That between twelve and one o'clock on Monday morning he was walking upon the high road from Bamber Bridge to Stock's Farm; and when he got near to the Grove Inn, on Fylde Road, he heard a noise before him, somewhere near the Rawstorne's Arms public house, of some persons quarrelling or fighting. Being afraid that if he went forward he might stand a chance of being ill-treated by the persons quarrelling, and whom he supposed to be drunk, he went down the Old Water Lane and came out again on the high road near to the gates of Mr. Taylor's factory. He there saw two men in the road – one lying down and the other standing over him; and he heard the latter exclaim, "What, hasn't t'had enough?" Going a little nearer, he saw this man try to lift the other up off the ground, but he did not succeed; and shortly after the man ran away. Billington then went towards the man who remained upon the ground, and the other man then returned, shouting out "Holloa! Who art thou? Where dost t'live? Where art t'going?" Billington replied that he was going home and lived at Mr. Miller's, when the other said, "Oh, is that thee, Charlie?" Billington then saw that the man was Henry Glover. They walked together a short distance, when Glover said, "Shall I go and punch him?" Billington replying, "No, you wouldn't punch a man when he is drunk?", and Glover responding , "Oh, he is only foxing." They then walked in company as far as Stock's Farm, where they parted; Glover telling Billington that "It was a bad job and he mustn't mention it."

On Tuesday morning Billington again met Glover who, in the company of constable Hindle, was going to attend the inquest on the body, and he crossed over to Billington and again wished him not to mention it.

Once Mr. Miller had heard this statement he deemed it his duty to make it known to the Borough Magistrates and he accordingly informed them of the whole transaction. Billington was subsequently examined by the Magistrates and instructions followed for the apprehension of Henry Glover, the son of a respectable farmer who was the tenant of Lea Hall Farm. The farmer's son was a man in his late twenties, of slender build, average height and fair complexion and when the constables called, he was at home. Being immediately taken into custody and informed that he was charged with the murder of Edward Latham, he showed little concern and merely remarked "It's all wrong. It's all false." Some clothing of Glover's was found upon which there were marks of blood.

Glover was subsequently brought before the Magistrates at the Town Hall and the statement of Billington was duly examined. The Defence Counsel attempted to undermine Billington's version of the events, however, the decision of the Magistrates was that Henry Glover should be committed for trial accused of the manslaugher of Edward Latham, who was a married man with a son and two daughters. After a brief consultation the Magistrates agreed to the Defence request of bail for Henry Glover, and he was bound over on the sum of £100. As he left the Town Hall the prisoner was followed by a large crowd of boys and 'children of a larger growth', who, in their anxiety to gratify their feelings of curiosity by a close inspection of the man's features, pressed upon him so much that he was compelled to return to the hall. Several policemen then escorted him a short distance and the mob soon afterwards dispersed.

Henry Glover appeared at Lancaster Spring Assizes towards the end of March, 1850 before Baron Alderson and he pleaded 'Not Guilty' to the manslaughter charge. Billington once again repeated his version of events and constable Hindle told how he had discovered the body of Edward Latham. The surgeon who carried out the post mortem was also called and repeated his view that the injuries had not been caused by one fall.

The Defence Counsel addressed the Jury in an eloquent manner, contending that it had never been shown that the man had died from injuries received from the prisoner. He attributed the death to the fall, and submitted that the evidence of Billington, on which the case rested, was not worthy of credence. After a consultation the Jury acquitted the prisoner. The court rose at six o'clock when the criminal business of the Assizes was terminated.

TO TAME THE DRUNKEN SOLDIERS

IN June, 1848, some five years after they had been commenced, the military Barracks at Fulwood were completed. The site is a portion of the old race course and is a mile and a quarter from the town centre in a north-easterly direction. The stone used in all the buildings was obtained from the Delph at Longridge and when completed the whole complex had cost just less than £138,000.

The arrival of the soldiers was not without its problems as the military men mingled with the citizens of the garrison town. In fact, it was necessary for two or three army pickets to nightly patrol the leading thoroughfares of the town to keep their comrades in hand.

The soldiers were often in conflict with both police and civilians. The troubles usually started on pay day and lasted until they had spent up. As many as twenty or thirty would gather in a beerhouse, and drink until they were mad drunk, at which point they would turn out spoiling for a fight. The general view was that they may have been good soldiers, but they were without a doubt, bad citizens.

The most notable incident involving both the soldiers and the police took place on the last day of November in 1881. On that particular Wednesday evening a number of soldiers were gathered at the Plumbers Arms, formerly the Fighting Cocks, a beerhouse situated at the bottom of Friargate.

The trouble began about eight o'clock when P.C. Thomas Swarbrick, who was passing the beerhouse, was approached by a woman who complained that a couple of soldiers had been in her house and that they had broken her mangle. A group of five of the soldiers were stood outside the public house and overheard her complaint, and the officer's enquiry as to whether the woman could recognise the men. She was unsure of their identity and the constable, sensing trouble, advised the men to disperse. They did not take kindly to the request and began pulling off their belts as they yelled to their comrades within the Inn to "Come out to the rescue." Out the fellows, numbering about thirty, rushed, some with sticks and others with their belts.

One of them immediately struck out at P.C. Swarbrick smashing five of his teeth with the first blow. The commotion soon gained the attention of the other constables in the Friargate area and as they made their singular attempts to intervene, they were treated violently by the soldiers. The first officer to rush to P.C. Swarbrick's aid was violently kicked and struck with belts, it taking him all his time to keep the blows, from the brass clasps of the belts, off his face.

It was next the turn of the biggest man in the police force, P.C. Richard Howard, commonly known as 'Red Dick', to enter the fray. As he approached the mob he roared out in his strong rough voice, "You rascals, you fancy you are going to carry the town because you are soldiers? What do you take us for? Go back you silly fools, or we will make you."

His intervention was short-lived, because no sooner had he squared up to the mob, than he was struck on the head from behind by a stick with a nob on. He at once crumpled to the ground insensible, dislocating his shoulder in the process.

Friargate was in a very excited state, and fearing the unruly mob, the shopkeepers hastened to put up their shutters. One of the constables was chased by a dozen soldiers and ended up seeking refuge in a tobacconist's shop in Fylde Street.

It was that time of evening when the night policemen were coming on to their beats and the day men going off duty, so it took the police some time to gather in numbers. When they did they showed the military men their efficiency and soon had them on the run. The running fight continued along Moor Lane, Garstang Road and Moor Park Avenue, as the soldiers retreated towards their Barracks.

The following morning at the Borough Police Court, nineteen soldiers stood before the Mayor, Edmund Birley, and the Magistrates. They were charged with committing a breach of the peace and assaulting the police. Among the witnesses was P.C. Swarbrick, who appeared with plaster covering wounds on his upper lip and forehead and P.C. Howard, who had his head bandaged and left arm in a sling.

Most of the proceedings on that day and the following days, were concerned with identification of the main culprits in the affray.

Eventually it was felt that there was sufficient evidence to proceed further against seven soldiers. Their ages ranged from nineteen to twenty-three and they belonged to the 27th and 108th Regiments.

As a result, the seven appeared at Preston Quarter Sessions early in January, 1882. The circumstances of the case were once again laid bare and at the conclusion of the evidence, the Jury returned 'Guilty' verdicts against all except one of the accused. It was felt that the participation in the disturbance of one of the prisoners could not be sufficiently established. The other six soldiers being informed that they were each sentenced to eight months imprisonment, with hard labour.

Preston's Chief Constable, Mr. Joseph Oglethorpe, was proud of the way his officers had handled the riotous behaviour of the soldiers. He retired with a pension in July, 1882 after spending ten years as the head of Preston's police force.

The model soldiers on parade at Fulwood Barracks – but off-duty they were a reckless lot

A FATAL FIRE IN CHURCH STREET

S HORTLY after one o'clock on the morning of Wednesday, March 31st, 1875 a fire broke out on the premises 119 Church Street, Preston. The building was occupied by James McNeil, a tailor and draper and had upper dwelling apartments, which extended over an adjoining shop of a neighbour, Mr. Compstay a tallow chandler.

The fire, when discovered, appeared to have obtained a complete hold of the whole interior of the building as flames were seen bursting through both the windows above and the crevices of the shutters and doorway below. The alarm was given by a chance passer-by, and was at once conveyed to the police station and the station of the fire brigade.

Meanwhile, attempts were made to alarm the inmates of the premises, but they found their escape by the staircase cut off. The flames had thoroughly mastered the whole of the interior of the shop, and had fastened upon the stairs. Driven thus back, Mr. McNeil and one of his sons, James Robert McNeil, aged 14, appeared at the front window over Mr. Compstay's shop and dropped into the street, fortunately without any personal injury.

They, too, aided in the general alarm, trying every means in their power to awaken the other sleepers. They were successful eventually in arousing the housekeeper, Mrs. Dewhurst, who also contrived to effect her escape in safety by dropping from the window onto the flags in the street below. It was impossible however to arouse the three other occupants of the building, or if the alarm had reached them they were finding it impossible to make their escape.

In this terrible state as to the fate of the remaining members of the family, the work of subduing the flames was steadily carried on. The premises being situated within a comparatively short distance of the Tithebarn Street fire brigade station, a staff of men with the hose reel and other appliances were soon on the spot. Water in ample force was at hand from adjacent mains, and several streams were soon directed into the interior of the building. The very intensity of the flames appeared to have aided the firemen in their efforts to extinguish the flames. For all the more combustible part of the material

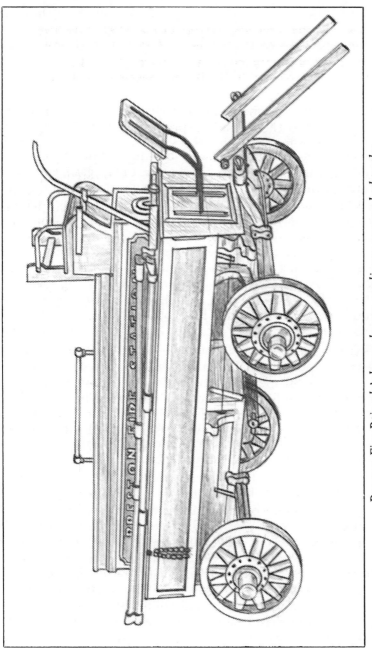

Preston Fire Brigade's horse-drawn appliance was rushed to the Church Street blaze

had at once been consumed and thus deprived of sustenance, the flames speedily became mastered. The fact, too, of the shop doors and windows being closed prevented the flames spreading with any great rapidity, owing to the lack of air. At the same time however, pent up as they were, their strength and the fierceness of their brief usurpation was all the greater.

In all half an hour sufficed to put out the fire. The work was carried on in almost painful quiet, as the terrible suspicion that several lives had been sacrificed gained ground every moment.

As soon as it was found safe to enter the premises, Superintendent Oglethorpe and Sergeant Copland of the fire brigade, entered the third storey of the building by an attic. They carried with them lanterns and their entry had scarcely been made when their worst fears were realised. A melancholy and harrowing sacrifice of life had resulted within the previous sad hour.

The dead bodies of Mr. McNeil's remaining three sons were discovered in varying positions. The first body which the searchers came across was that of Charles McNeil, a fine young man of 22 years of age. He was found lying upon his bed in the attic, over Mr. Compstay's shop, quite dead. The probability was that the alarm from the street failed utterly to arouse him. It was believed that a stalwart young fellow like him would have made light work of escaping from a building with a window opening at hand.

The next body discovered was that of the second son, John, aged 19 years. This unfortunate youth seemed as though he had been partly aroused from his sleep and to have made slight efforts to escape before he was overcome by the smoke and flames. He was lying on the same bed as his brother, or rather partially so; for when found his legs were resting upon the bed and the upper part of his body was resting on the floor.

The youngest son, Alexander, a lad of 10 years, was found lying upon the staircase leading into the house part of his father's residence. This poor lad, who slept in the same room with his father, appeared to have been effectually aroused, only to find his retreat cut off at the stairs. Shortly after the outbreak the lad was seen at the window from where his father and one of his brothers escaped, but he had appeared too frightened to drop into the street. He then disappeared and, as was evident, and too plain, in attempting to get away by the staircase, he was met by the flames and fell a victim of their fury.

Neither of the two elder brothers was burned, death in their cases having resulted from suffocation. The boy however, was found to have been burned about the face.

Stretchers were at once fetched from the police station and the bodies of Mr. McNeil's three sons were conveyed to the dead house at the fire brigade station.

The Inquest was held on the Wednesday evening and an attempt was made to find the cause of the lamentable disaster. The general belief was that the outbreak of fire had arisen from the dropping of a live coal or cinder from the fire grate. When the family had retired on the Tuesday evening a brisk fire was burning in the kitchen grate. Tuesday had been 'washing day' and some of the linen had been left to dry in front of the grate. This led to the supposition that an accidental spark may have set the linen ablaze, or that linen first dried may have become scorched and ultimately burst into flames.

Inspection in daylight had revealed the awful fury of the blaze which resulted in the heart-rending loss of life.

A heavy stock of cloth was kept on the premises, all of which was found almost reduced to tinder and the loss on that account was said to have reached £2,000, only part of which was covered by insurance. The furniture of the kitchen was reduced to ashes, scarcely an article being recognisable as having been of domestic matter or use.

Adjoining Mr. McNeil's kitchen there was an extensive warehouse belonging to Mr. Compstay and this was stored with material of a most inflammable nature. The firemen were praised for preventing the spread of the blaze and for their great energy.

The survivors of the fire were obliged to relive their nightmare before the Coroner. Mr. McNeil, a widower, told of his efforts to arouse his family after waking due to a feeling of suffocation. Rushing on to the landing he had called out that the house was on fire. Almost overcome by smoke he was forced to make his exit.

Mr. McNeil lived in the premises with his housekeeper, four sons and two daughters. Fortunately on the tragic night the daughters were staying away from home.

The Coroner regretted that he had found it necessary to call Mr. McNeil to give evidence and he expressed his deepest sympathy.

The Jury, after a brief consultation, returned a verdict of 'Accidental Death' on the three victims of the Church Street fire.

PERILOUS PROGRESS ON THE VIADUCT

PRESTON, due to its geographical situation, was very much at the forefront of railway development. The first railway in these parts being the one which opened at the end of October, 1838 connecting Preston with Wigan.

As a result Preston became known as a reliable place of work for the breed known as the railroad labourer. The influx of these hired hands by their hundreds did not go unnoticed and in January, 1839 the 'Preston Pilot' newspaper under the heading 'The Railroad Labourer' described the town's new inhabitants thus:

The navigator appears to belong to no country; he wanders from one public work to another – now alone, then with a party of two or three; and as long as he has sixpence in his pocket seems contented. Yet he sets so little value on the earnings of his slavish employment as never to be at ease unless squandering his money; although well paid for his labour.

Go where he will, he finds some of his comrades whom he has met before and inquires as to their mode of living, and the wages they were paid since they last met.

His attire is peculiar – on his head he wears a kind of white felt hat, the brim of which is turned up all round and generally a tobacco pipe is stuck in his hand, and it is of some glaring colour. He usually sports a shooting jacket with white buttons, a scarlet plush waistcoat of large dimensions, sometimes a brightly coloured neckerchief adorns his neck. His trousers are invariably corduroy, retained in their position by a leather strap around the waist, and tied and buttoned at the knee. Sometimes he wears white or grey worsted stockings which reach up to his knees and high laced boots of strong construction complete his dress.

A small smock frock is slung at the back when he travels and in this he carries whatever else he has in the world. In some things he makes attempts at taste, such as the dressing of the hair, by wearing one or more ringlets on each side of his face. Generally he knows of no other pleasure or domestic comfort than that which is afforded at a public house or beer shop, happy to be brawling or drinking with his companions after the toils of the day.

Of course their work was hard and hazardous and great interest was taken in the constructions that developed as a result of their labours.

By the beginning of 1840 great local curiosity was shown as the Preston and Wyre Railway reached its final stages. Interest being particularly intense over the construction of the viaduct linking the

Tulketh hill and the high lands at the Maudland. To complete the line from Tulketh Brow to the Preston terminus a tremendous feat of 19th century engineering was in progress. The immense viaduct with its twelve arches, was being constructed entirely of brick, with support pillars of brick.

Week by week another arch would take shape as the army of bricklayers kept to their task. Indeed, all seemed to be going according to plan until the first Tuesday in May, 1840. On that particular afternoon the bricklayers were busy constructing the ninth arch from the Preston end, when suddenly disaster struck. Just after three o'clock that day, with the arch half finished and fourteen men and two boys at work, the framework, or centre, gave way and fell, with a sudden and frightful crash. Hurtling to the ground, a distance of thirty to forty feet, went some eighty tons of bricks and mortar and with it went the unfortunate persons working on the arch. The men and boys being precipitated headlong to the earth, several of them being literally buried in the rubble.

The scene which presented itself after the columns of dust had settled was particularly harrowing. The poor sufferers on the heap of ruins crawling about and shrieking from the combined effects of their terror and the agony produced by their various injuries.

Assistance was promptly and amply rendered and it was ascertained that two lads and three of the men who had fallen had miraculously escaped with only trifling injuries. The rest though, were shockingly mutilated, and all of them were severely cut and bruised.

One poor fellow, a fine young man named Edward Lewis, was so dreadfully injured that he died within a few minutes of being rescued from the rubble. The remaining sufferers were at once conveyed to the House of Recovery where they received the skilful and zealous attention of surgeons Holden, Dixon, Naylor and Howitt.

Over the next few days the death toll was to rise to four, and the surgeons reported that of the other patients a number would be cripples for life.

An inquest held into the death of Edward Lewis was held at the Town Hall and witnesses told how the deceased had been carried from the scene to the Wheatsheaf public house, and that by the time they got there he was dead.

The general opinion was that all care and diligence were exercised by the workmen in the construction of the arch and one expert stated that, with his experience, he considered the centre of the arch

Preston to Wyre Railway Viaduct – Tulketh Brow. Week by week another arch took shape, and then on an afternoon in May 1840, one of the arches came tumbling down with fatal consequences

Despite fears over the structure, it still stands today

quite strong enough for the weight it had to bear. However, a carpenter who was called said that in his opinion the cause of the accident was that the longitudinal timbers had not been strong enough to support the pressure of the arches. The jury seemed not to want to attach blame and they declined the Coroner's offer of further witnesses and recorded a verdict of 'Accidental Death'.

The following week, as if to emphasis the dangers of the work, two more accidents occurred. In one a labourer, who was removing soil from a waggon, was crushed when the waggon upturned upon him. The poor fellow being rushed to the House of Recovery with broken legs. The other accident took place close to the fallen viaduct arch, when a large piece of timber gave way and fell upon the leg of a labourer.

Despite the tragic setbacks the building of the railway continued and the remaining arches of the Tulketh viaduct were added in time for the public opening of the Preston to Fleetwood line on Wednesday, July 15th, 1840. Not surprisingly, the opening created a very powerful and lively interest amongst the residents of Preston and, indeed, the people at all the places en route to Fleetwood. At that time there was only one line of rails on the 19-mile route and it had cost in the region of £260,000 to construct.

The train left the North Union Railway station, at Preston, shortly before midday and among the numerous dignitaries aboard were a number of the principal inhabitants of Preston. Thousands of spectators converged on the station to witness the departure, flags and banners of every hue were proudly waved and two excellent music bands contributed their exhilarating influence to the proceedings.

All the way to the Tulketh viaduct the road was thickly lined by spectators of both sexes and of all classes and conditions, who lustily and loudly cheered the train along its course.

A rumour had gained great swell that as the train rumbled across the viaduct, the bridge would surely collapse. So as the train reached that point there was a feeling of dark and dismal foreboding amongst the passengers as to the possible fate that awaited them, an outward show of gaiety masking their inner fears.

The viaduct was however, traversed gallantly and safely and when they reached the other side the passengers were greeted by a loud and enthusiastic cheer from the thousands who had gathered to lament over the 'downfall' of the train.

From Tulketh the train proceeded to Kirkham where hundreds more cheered the travellers and then on to Poulton, where another warm welcome was given. Then it was on to Fleetwood, over the embankment, where the crowds had gathered in their thousands. As the passengers descended from the train, four times four rounds of cheerings greeted them and the bands began to play.

The journey had taken barely an hour and that afternoon the special guests were taken on a cruise and then treated to a magnificent banquet. The railway had been the brainchild of Sir Peter Hesketh Fleetwood and amongst the dignitaries who dined was George Stephenson 'the father of the railways'.

At about a quarter to seven the guests left the banqueting hall and proceeded, amid the playing of the band and firing of guns, to the waiting railway carriages. The train consisted of nine carriages and was soon making its way safely over the embankment.

Alas, a day of celebration was soon to be marred by tragedy. In the second carriage from the front was a man by the name of William Dean, who hailed from Preston and who was, by trade, a tailor. He had arrived at Fleetwood sober, but as he boarded the train for his return journey he seemed, by those who knew him, to be somewhat the worse for liquor.

For some inexplicable reason he ended up on top of one of the first-class carriages. From his precarious position he lifted up his hand to beckon the engineer to stop the train. Before the driver could respond William Dean had fallen from the carriage.

When the engine was brought to a halt a number of people hurried down the track to where the body of Dean lay. It appeared that a number of wheels had traversed over him and his head was completely severed from his body. The body of the unfortunate man was conveyed to Thornton where the following morning an inquest was held, which returned an 'Accidental Death' verdict.

The painful and untoward occurrence had detained the train for some twenty minutes and it was ten minutes past eight o'clock when the train arrived back at Preston. Sadly a day of gaiety and gladness had ended with an air of gloom hanging over it, with another death on the railways to be added to the mounting toll.

At least the viaduct had survived its test and in the month that followed no less than 20,000 passengers were carried on that rail.

STABBING OF A PRESTON VICAR

IN 1973 St. Paul's Church in Preston closed its doors for the last time and the parish was amalgamated with St. Jude's Church. The closure brought to an end a chapter that had begun in the month of October, 1823 when the Vicar of Preston, the Rev. Carus Wilson had laid the foundation stone. The church was built on land formerly known as 'The Park' and which was donated by Samuel Pole Shawe. In all the church cost £6,500 to build, and along with its sister church St. Peter's was paid for with funds provided by the Government to commemorate the 'Battle of Waterloo'.

The vicar of St. Paul's had walked briskly down Friargate into a deathly struggle – hours later the nineteenth century newspaper boy proclaims news of the vicar's terrifying ordeal.

Throughout its century and a half of existence the church was blessed with a number of dedicated and enthusiastic clergy, four of which were to rise to the position of Bishop in their later years. One such clergyman was the Rev. Riley who, towards the end of 1894, left the parish to travel to Western Australia to become the Bishop of Perth.

When his intentions were made known the Vicar of Preston, Canon Rawdon, invited the Rev. Henry Henn to become the next vicar of St. Paul's. At the time he was in attendance at Trinity Hall, Cambridge, but he had little hesitation in accepting the position offered, which meant a return to Preston where he had spent four happy years, including a spell as curate at the Parish Church.

The parish was a thriving one with successful Sunday schools and a large and devoted congregation who welcomed their new vicar with enthusiasm. He soon settled in to parish life and built a genuine affection with those around him.

Not surprisingly therefore, his congregation and, indeed, the town where shocked to hear of an incident involving the vicar in April, 1896. The date was in fact the 21st of April, it was a Tuesday, and the Rev. Henn, as he often did, went for a lunchtime visit to the town centre. On this particular day the vicar made his way to Friargate intending to visit 138, Friargate, the shop of Mr. Ianson, stationer.

Also in the town centre that day was a man called Henry Walmsley, a forty-year-old labourer, who was acting in a most peculiar manner. He was observed by the Rev. Henn, to be running along with his arms held up and shouting to the heavens. The vicar puzzled by the man's behaviour turned to John Jackson, an employee of the Harris Free Library, who was passing alongside and said, "Is the man mad?" The library employee replying, "I cannot tell you, but he looks as if he were a bit dotty."

The Rev. Henn, who was walking at a brisk pace, then continued on his way down to the stationer's shop and John Jackson's attention remained fixed on the antics of the labourer, Walmsley. He was seen to dart from one side of the road to the other and when he got to Orchard Street corner, he slipped and his hat fell. Dusting himself down after his fall, he then walked for a little before making a sudden dash towards Mr. Ianson's shop, which the Rev. Henn had entered only a minute earlier.

The vicar was speaking to the shop keeper across the counter with his back to the door, when he felt himself suddenly struck on

After entering a Friargate shop the Rev. Henn was involved in a deathly struggle.

the right side of the neck. He fell forward on to the counter, and as he struggled to rise, he realised he was being attacked by a man with a knife in his right hand. A scuffle then developed and the Rev. Henn tried to protect himself with his umbrella, with which he succeeded in warding off several blows delivered with the knife in the direction of his face.

When Walmsley's intentions had become apparent the shopkeeper sprang over the counter to the vicar's aid and he was at once joined by John Jackson, who after observing developments from outside the shop, rushed to the scene. The two men set about disarming the vicar's assailant whose weapon was a tackler's knife which he held by the handle with a fearful grip. Only after a considerable struggle did they manage to wrench it from his grasp and, disarmed, the man was held until a police officer on patrol in Friargate arrived inside the shop.

The Rev. Henn had reacted quickly to the attack upon him and when examined he was seen to have a deep cut in his neck about two inches long. He also had three slight scratches on his head and other thrusts of the knife had cut through his waistcoat and collar. After receiving medical assistance at the police station and relating the details of the incident he returned to his vicarage home.

That afternoon Henry Walmsley, who appeared to have been suffering from the effects of drink, was formally charged with unlawfully wounding Henry Henn, clerk in holy orders.

The following afternoon he was brought before the Magistrates, whose chairman was Mr. E. H. Booth. The proceedings raised a great deal of public interest and eyes were on the two principal figures in the case. The prisoner stood stolidly throughout, guarded by a policeman. He appeared quite cool and collected, in complete contrast to his excited demeanour the previous day. It was reported that he lived with his wife and children at 17, Pole Street and that he had in the past served in India as a soldier.

A seat was provided for the Rev. Henn who appeared to move his neck stiffly, as if suffering from the wound which had been inflicted there. A couple of superficial wounds were also visible on the scalp of his head.

The evidence was laid before the Magistrates in an orderly manner and the Rev. Henn gave an account of the assault upon his person. Under questioning he also stated that the prisoner and his wife and daughters were in fact parishioners. The vicar informing the gathering that Walmsley's wife was a member of his congregation, although he did not know the accused.

Before being committed for trial at Manchester Assizes, the prisoner simply said, "I was under the influence of drink, and have nothing more to add."

On the last Tuesday of April, 1896 Henry Walmsley stood trial before Mr. Justice Grantham and the Jury found him 'Guilty'. The Chief Constable of Preston, Major Little, at this point came forward to speak for the prisoner, informing the court that Walmsley had served six years in the army and had suffered from sunstroke while in India. He had been discharged with a good character and had over the years been a hard-working man.

When his Lordship passed sentence he said that in normal circumstances he would have inflicted a long term of penal servitude. He also reminded the prisoner that but for the interposition of providence he would have been standing before him on a capital charge of murder. He then announced that the sentence was one of twelve months imprisonment, with hard labour.

The Rev. Henn soon recovered from his ordeal and he remained as vicar of St. Paul's until 1902. Some twenty five years later, by which time he was the Bishop of Burnley he recalled the event in a summary of his time at St. Paul's stating, "Some will remember an attempt on my life made by a poor crazy man which served to make evident the wealth of affection of the dear people among whom I lived."

Postscript:
After its closure, the church building remained empty for eight years and its future looked bleak. At that point the derelict structure was bought and renovated, for the use of Red Rose Radio, and is now home to the tuneful melodies of local broadcasting.

THE DAY THE GRAVE FELL IN

IN July, 1849 the 'Preston Guardian' published a letter from a resident of the town on the subject of graveyards. The writer informed the public that the town could not be healthy as long as there were seventeen church and chapel grounds continually reeking with animal fluids. He had calculated that no less than 40,000 bodies had been interred within the precincts of the town during a period of fifty years.

In particular he drew the public attention to the St. Paul's burial ground where at one corner he had found a large open grave which had been the cause of pestilence. In that open grave seven coffins had been deposited and it was intended to eventually hold twenty five.

In the summer of 1849, the St. Paul's burial ground came in for much criticism. It was claimed that the stench from the mass graves was unbearable

Twelve months previously, after one pit had been filled with coffins, the grave diggers proceeded to open another without leaving any space of land between; so that instead of putting in sideboards to prevent the earth from falling in upon them, the coffins of the closed grave were made to answer that purpose.

He then went on to relate how corruption had begun to escape from the decomposed bodies, and that the stench had been so great that when the wind was in a westerly direction, he had been compelled to keep the windows and doors of his nearby dwelling closed in order to prevent the pestiferous odour from entering. By his calculations, the writer estimated that up to forty coffins were placed in an open grave designed to accept twenty five, and he observed that the final coffins deposited were near the level of the original earth.

To his mind it was a shameful and disgraceful mode of disposing of the bodies of the poor, while the rich continued to be buried in their family vaults. His hope was that soon the remains of rich and poor alike would be deposited together in an open cemetery at a distance from the town. No longer then would the health of Prestonians deteriorate due to the poisonous exhalations arising from church and chapel burial grounds.

CHURCH BURIAL GROUNDS IN PRESTON.

To the Editor of the Guardian.

SIR,—May I request you to favour me with the insertion of the following evidence of myself and others relative to the burial ground of St. Paul's Church, and forwarded by letter to Mr. Clark, the Sanitary Inspector, during his visit to Preston:—

"THE EVIDENCE OF J. CATTERALL—I have lived in St. Paul's-square two years and four months. We had not resided here more than one month before my wife and daughters began to complain of repeated nauseous smells. At first they thought that these must arise from some dead animal carcass, or something of the kind on the Moor near to our dwelling; but after being satisfied this was not the case, we soon ascertained most satisfactorily that the effluvium proceeded from the overcrowded graveyard at the east end of St. Paul's Church, opposite to our dwelling. We have at times been compelled to leave the parlour and retire to the back kitchen on account of the deleterious and health-destroying gas which constantly contaminates the atmosphere.

"Mr. RILEY's evidence is as follows:—I lived in St. Paul's-square upwards of three years. My principal reason for removing was on account of the very bad smells which came from the churchyard. Indeed, my wife was always ill during our stay there. We have enjoyed good health since we left; and, moreover, my neighbours, Mrs. Capstick's family, who formerly resided at the west end of the church, have enjoyed superior, yea, good health, since they ceased living and breathing so near thousands of dead bodies. Indeed, Dr. Norris told them they could not have good health while they lived where they did. I am willing to give this evidence orally before you.

"Mr. R. WILKINSON has suffered through ill-health for the last fifteen or sixteen months. His illness commenced during the time he lived in St. Paul's-square, but he has removed some time since. He can give some striking and telling facts in reference to this churchyard. He has had much conversation with the assistant sexton on the interments there, more especially as it regards the poor being buried in layers at the east end; but considering the short stay he is likely to have here, and from other considerations, he feels a backwardness in giving evidence.

Mr. Sergeant WILLIAMS, inspector of nuisances for this town, is in possession of the evidence of Mr. Critchley, formerly a resident in this square. Mr. Clerkson, and indeed many others, could give similar facts as above stated. Mr. C. prevented a family from coming into this square on account of the injurious and offensive smells so common in its locality. The above, Mr. Editor, is a copy sent to Mr. Clark, the inspector, in reference to St. Paul's burial ground. It is true I have omitted many important facts in the report, such as the following:—Previous to my exposing the state of this church-yard, the sexton left open the big hole both night and day, and even so late as the first Saturday evening of this year, it was left open; that is, the boards were not thrown over the hole, and it has, at this moment, only a few boards put over the mouth. If I am right in my numbers, no fewer than 150 have been buried close to my house since the first Sunday of this year up to the present date. Mr. Clark, after having read over my report, said he felt satisfied that it could not be otherwise than correct, and most emphatically added that the yards were in a most disgraceful state. My report was presented to Mr. Clark during the time he was inspecting St. Paul's church-yard.

Yours respectfully, J. CATTERALL.

Preston Guardian 16th June, 1849

He finished his contribution to the paper by stating, "Our cities are built upon corpses; the very air we breathe is laden with the dust of former ages; and its murmurings are the sighs of antiquity."

Four years later at the beginning of August, 1853, the matter of large open graves for the burial of the poorer inhabitants once more came into the public glare. On the first Thursday of that month, a most appalling accident occurred in the churchyard of St. Peter's on the eastern side of Fylde Road.

The man at the centre of the incident was William Calderbank, a 47-year-old-labourer, who was employed under the instructions of the sexton of the Parish Church, who had the management of the graves in St. Peter's burial ground. At midday that Thursday, William Calderbank met the sexton at St. Peter's Church and was given instructions to sweep the gravestones and to take a bier to Christ Church Place. There was to be a funeral in the afternoon, and the sexton informed him that the grave had already been prepared, and that he himself would return prior to the arrival of the funeral party.

The grave had in fact been made the previous week and was referred to as the 'big hole' being originally 24 feet deep. During its first seven days, several coffins had been deposited and the five feet wide opening had been reduced to 21 feet deep, with the sides supported by a wooden framing. Although an open grave, intended to continue so until filled with bodies, it was always covered at the top with planks.

Later that afternoon another labourer, Frederick Hothersall, was sent on an errand to the St. Peter's churchyard. He arrived at about twenty minutes before two o'clock and as he entered the burial area, he observed a large volume of sand rising in the air from the open grave. By the side of the grave he observed a coat, which he recognised as belonging to William Calderbank. The grave was all closed in, the wooden framework had disappeared and the hole was filled in to within three feet of the ground level.

He immediately ran for assistance and along with three other persons he began clearing the grave out. They toiled for five anxious hours before reaching the body of their colleague, who was quite dead when found. So completely had William Calderbank been embedded in the sand, that it was an hour after his head was laid bare that his lifeless body could be removed.

The news of the fearful tragedy had spread quickly and a large crowd had assembled by the time the corpse was removed from its

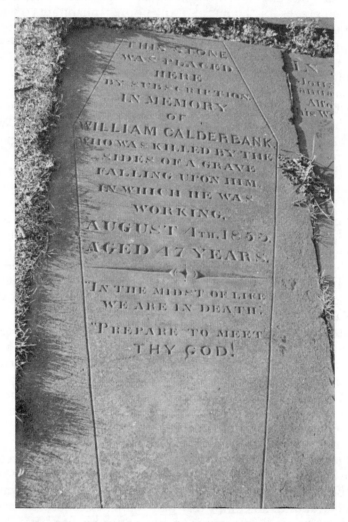

*In St. Peter's graveyard, an inscribed gravestone
records the tragic end of William Calderbank*

premature grave. When the inquest was held into the man's death, a verdict of 'Accidental Death' was recorded. For some unknown reason he had entered the grave and, whilst he was there, the supporting timbers had given way. He had been given no instructions either to go into it or interfere with it in any way.

The inquest over, William Calderbank, a single man, was interred in St. Peter's churchyard and his last resting place is marked by a flat stone slab which records his burial 'alive' on that fateful Thursday in 1853.

Two years later in July, 1855 the town of Preston got its long-awaited cemetery on the eastern side of town in Ribbleton. When the cemetery was opened, all the burial grounds in Preston, with the exception of those connected with St. Ignatius and St. Augustine's Catholic Churches, were closed. St. Ignatius's burial ground closing at the end of the year and St. Augustine's interments ending twelve months later. The first interment of at the new cemetery was that of bricksetter's daughter, six-year-old Elizabeth Frances Christian on the 3rd of July, 1855, in the Church of England part.

The general opinion of the nineteenth-century visitor to Preston Cemetery was that the walks are good; the ground well cared for; and in summer time with its trees, shrubs and flowers, the place is quite beautiful.

INTERMENTS IN PRESTON DURING THE LAST SEVEN YEARS.		
	Number Interred.	Burial Ground.
Saint John's	847	3700 sq. yards.
„ James's	10	506 „
Christ Church	36	2316 „
Saint George's	34	1188 „
„ Peter's	2535	6945 „
„ Paul's	3579	5550 „
„ Thomas's	13	1490 „
„ Mary's	13	2219 „
Trinity Church	260	2706 „
	7327	25620 sq. yards.

CATHOLIC BURIAL GROUNDS.		
	Adults.	Under 10 years.	Total.
Saint Ignatius's	613	937	1550
„ Augustine's	267	329	596
„ Wilfred's	501	421	922
	1381	1687	3068

DISSENTING CHAPELS' BURIAL GROUNDS.	
	Number interred.
Vauxhall-road	9
Friends' Burial Ground	30
Grimshaw-street	118
Unitarian Burial Ground	23
Leeming-street Burial Ground	48—228

SUMMARY.	
Total Established Churches	7327
„ Catholics	3068
„ Dissenters	228
	10023

Mr. John Catterall, who has furnished the above, remarks that St. John's Burial Ground has been used for such for 910 years.

Interments in Preston – seven year period ending 1849

LIVING IN THE SHADOW OF THE GALLOWS

FROM the beginning of the nineteenth century there was always great curiosity among the residents of Preston in the twice-yearly Assizes Court held at Lancaster Castle.

Up until the close of the eighteenth century the execution of convicted criminals at Lancaster had been carried out at a place known as Gallows Moor, near to the site of Christ Church. To there the condemned were transported in a cart, being seated on their coffins for the journey. Often the cart had been laden with four, eight or even ten unhappy malefactors.

The new century though had heralded great changes at Lancaster Castle, with government funds being provided for a new Crown Court, suitable for the trials of all Lancashire's wrongdoers. In our county, the sternest code of morality was administered without a wavering hand. Many were taken to Lancaster Castle chained and shackled and placed in the new County Jail to await their appearance in the Assizes Court.

The court soon gained a fearful reputation and it was claimed that more persons stood in the dock to receive sentence of death, than in any other court in the Kingdom. In one four-year period, starting in 1816, no less than 240 criminals received the dreaded sentence. However the great majority of them received the clemency of the Crown and were reprieved before the judges left the town. Their substitute sentences being anything from transportation to life imprisonment.

Many though, received 'a short shrift and a stout rope', the pattern having been set at the opening assizes in 1800 when six persons were executed and in the March Assizes of the following year, eleven suffered death. As the years passed by, the murderer, the highway robber, the utterer of forged notes, the horse stealer, the burglar, the rapist and various other felons had ended their days looking out from Hanging Corner.

In March 1828, Preston's own Jane Scott stood on the public gallows which faced the churchyard, to be despatched from this life.

Not surprisingly, therefore, much local interest was displayed in March, 1834 when an article appeared in the 'Preston Pilot' newspaper once again mentioning arsenic, murder and the threat of the gallows for a woman. This time the dramatic happenings had taken place at Hurst Green, a hamlet not too distant from this town.

The woman concerned was 25-year-old Mary Holden and she stood accused of the wilful murder of her husband, Roger Holden, aged 40. His death had occurred on the 26th of February after a sudden and dramatic failure of his health. The couple had been married for six years, during which time the wife had two children, only one of which was still living at the time of the alleged murder.

Following the inquest various information became public knowledge about the couple and the circumstances of Roger Holden's death. It appeared that the pair had lived upon very bad terms together. She being somewhat younger than her spouse, was suspected by him of an improper intimacy with some other man. He felt she had a particularly overweening fondness for young company, while she complained of his ill-treatment of her, when in liquor.

Upon one occasion about three weeks before his death, during one of their mutual recriminations, she was heard to say that, bad as she had been, she would be still worse and would play a trick he was not aware of. This was understood at the time to have reference to an intention on her part to prostitute herself.

Apparently on the evening of his death, at around eight o'clock, Roger Holden had visited the barn of Alice Chippendale, not far from his home. While there, he had complained of being unwell, saying that he felt ill all over, as if he had been 'nettled' in his bowels.

A local labourer had found it necessary to carry Roger Holden back to his home, as he was unable to walk. When they arrived at the house the distraught husband pointed at his wife and accused her of poisoning him.

His wife was dismissive of his comments, replying, "He's always laying something to me, and now he says I've poisoned him."

Those who had helped the husband home then carried him up to his bedroom, where they attempted to make him comfortable. His wife appeared totally indifferent to her spouse's condition, not even bothering to climb the stairs to enquire as to his welfare.

While lying on what would be his death bed, the husband told his companions that he had suspected his wife of poisoning him on a couple of previous occasions. Prior to visiting the barn, he had helped himself to a cup of coffee from the pot upon the stove. He therefore asked one of those present to go and examine the teapot.

On doing so, the man observed that the teapot had recently been washed out and the coffee dregs thrown away. However, a close examination of the spout of the pot revealed that it was lined with traces of a whitish powder, some of which could also be detected under the ledge of the lid.

By half past ten that night Roger Holden was dead and immediately suspicion was attached to his wife. Conversation took place between Mary Holden and those present at her home that night and, during it, she admitted that she had placed a portion of some arsenic in the pot with the intention of destroying her husband. She said she had obtained the poison as flea powder about a week earlier and she attempted to palliate and satisfy her conscience by asserting that she did not give him the pot to drink from, nor direct him to it. When the body was subjected to a post mortem examination, a considerable amount of arsenic was found in the stomach and the conclusion reached that death resulted from that cause. The Inquest Jury had no hesitation in finding Mary Holden guilty and as a result the Coroner committed her to Lancaster Castle for trial.

The following week a notice appeared in the 'Preston Pilot' announcing the forthcoming Lancaster March Assizes for 1834. Justice acted swiftly in those far off days and there was great speculation as to the likely outcome of Mary Holden's trial.

This particular Assizes was held before Mr. Justice Taunton and besides those charged with robbery, counterfeit coining, assault, rape, bigamy and manslaughter, there were eight cases with charges of 'Wilful Murder'.

The first week was spent on dealing with the lesser crimes and the imposing of various terms of imprisonment and transportation for those found guilty. Then, on the Monday morning of the second week, Mary Holden was placed in the dock.

She appeared to be a decent looking woman and she seemed to manifest considerable indifference to her situation. Various witnesses testified as to the state of her marriage, her indifference to her husband's condition and to her purchase of the poison. By the time the prosecution case was complete the evidence was stacked high against the woman.

Mary Holden was not represented by Counsel and when called upon for her defence, she said, "I never gave him, and I never would

4

LANCASTER MARCH ASSIZES, 1834.
NOTICE IS HEREBY GIVEN,

THAT the PRISONERS for TRIAL at the ASSIZES, commencing at LANCASTER, on SATURDAY the 8th day of MARCH next, will be classed in the Calendar in the following order:—

1st—All Criminals (not being for Murder, but including those prosecuted by the Bank and the Mint,) from Salford Hundred.

2d—The like from West-Derby and Leyland Hundreds.

3d—The like from all other parts of the County.

4th—Criminals for Murder.

And that the Grand Jury will proceed upon the Indictments against those of the First Class on Monday the 10th day of March, those of the Second Class on Tuesday the 11th of March, and those of the Third and Fourth Classes on Wednesday the 12th day of March next.

And that in default of a due observance of these regulations, neither the Attorneys nor the Witnesses will be allowed their expenses; and that no expenses will be allowed to them for their attendance previous to the day on which they are to appear before the Grand Jury, excepting for the day of travelling to Lancaster.

And Notice is hereby also given,

That at the said Assizes, the Causes will be entered and tried in the following order:—

1st List—Containing all Causes wherein the official residence of the Plaintiffs' Attorneys (or of the Plaintiffs themselves, when suing in person) is within the Hundred of West Derby, and places out of the County.

2d—Containing all Causes wherein such residence is within the Hundreds of Lonsdale, Amounderness, Blackburn, and Leyland.

3d—Containing all Causes wherein such residence is within the Hundred of Salford.

THOMAS BIRCHALL, Undersheriff.

Sheriff's Office, Preston, 18th February, 1834.

In the 'Preston Pilot' newspaper the forthcoming assizes were announced

MURDER.

James Walker, Richard Walker, Wm. Walker, and George Bretherton, charged with the wilful murder of N. Brooks, at Elton, near Bury.

Ann Pouder, charged with the wilful murder of her new-born male bastard child, at Liverpool.

John Wilson, charged with the wilful murder of Edmund Martin, at Liverpool.

William Taylor, charged with the wilful murder of Mary Ann Benson, at Liverpool.

William Kelsey, charged with the wilful murder of Sarah Davies, at Manchester.

John Gilburn, charged with the wilful murder of Joseph Tomkinson, at Manchester.

Richard Riley, charged with the wilful murder of Alice and Betty Riley, at Over Darwen.

Mary Holden, charged with the wilful murder of her husband, Roger Holden, at Hurst-green.

Mary Holden was listed amongst those facing murder charges

113

have given him poison. I put the stuff into the teapot with an intention to sprinkle for fleas and he by mistake got it. He partook of it and never said anything, nor did I hear of his being ill until somebody came in and told me. I had no idea of his taking it, for he was not in the habit of drinking out of the pot."

When Mr. Justice Taunton summed up the case he told the Jury to be aware of the punishment that awaited a 'Guilty' verdict. Informing them that they must be well satisfied of the accused woman's guilt before pronouncing a 'Guilty' verdict. After going over the evidence he told them that it all hinged on whether the woman had placed the poison in the teapot with an intention to poison her husband.

At the conclusion of the summing up, the prisoner begged that she might be allowed to call two of the debtors on her behalf, but when called they had nothing to say in her favour.

The Jury immediately found her 'Guilty' and His Lordship having put on the black cap, proceeded to pass sentence of death upon her. He stated that the murder was clearly premeditated, as she had purchased the deadly poison a week before it was taken by the victim. He then urged her to make amends by her penitence and contrition and by an acknowledgement of her crime.

His Lordship concluded by informing Mary Holden that she would be hanged on Wednesday morning next, and buried within the precincts of the prison. The prisoner was then removed from the dock and as she walked with a firm step to the penitentiary she was heard to utter the words, "My Lord, have mercy on me."

On the morning of her execution, Wednesday March 19th, she seemed to feel the awfulness of her situation more keenly than at any former period. Less than two days after being condemned she was to be hanged and she became overwhelmed by her impending fate. Despite being dreadfully agitated not a tear was observed to flow from her eyes.

Her last few minutes were spent in the chapel to which she was transported in a sedan chair, in order to avoid the gaze of the debtors in the prison yard. Two female attendants remained with her as she made her final devotions and when the dreaded hour of eight o'clock arrived she walked to the scaffold quite calm and collected.

After the rope had been fastened to the chain around the beam, by hangman Edward Barlow, her attendants embraced her and walked away. She then cried out, "Lord, relieve me out of my misery." The attendant chaplain then read a short prayer, which she repeated aloud; at the conclusion of which the drop fell. She struggled violently for a few moments and then life was extinct.

In the space of three weeks Mary Holden had committed her crime, been tried and convicted and finally executed. She had been cut off in the prime of life; she had been a decent looking woman of middle stature, slightly muscular, of unprepossessing appearance, with nothing in her countenance to indicate a ferocious disposition.

An hour later her body was removed to the interior of the gaol and prepared for its interment within the precincts of the prison. The crowd assembled was not as great as on other 'hanging days', due mainly to it being a working day in the town. Of those who were present to witness the end of Mary Holden, a large proportion were females and young children.

That day, the Assizes court only resumed its business at ten o'clock owing to the execution. Fortunately, none of the other murder trials at that Assizes led to execution, although those whose committals for murder were changed to manslaughter received a variety of punishments including transportation for life.

The following year part of the Assizes for Lancashire were transferred to Liverpool, and thirty years later another portion was moved to Manchester. The last public execution that took place at Lancaster Castle was that of Preston tailor, Stephen Burke, in March 1865, for the murder of his wife. Ten years later in August, 1875 another Preston wife killer, Mark Fiddler, suffered the same fate, although this time the execution was carried out within the walls of Lancaster Castle.

By the time of those executions the Castle's resident executioner, Edward Barlow, had long since passed away and the dreaded sentence was carried out by the Official Executioner. In the case of Stephen Burke, William Calcraft performed the deed and his successor William Marwood ended the life of Mark Fiddler.

Marwood, the long-drop hangman

THE career of William Calcraft, executioner ended in 1874 (see Book 2) when he performed an execution at Newgate and he was succeeded by William Marwood who became known as the 'long-drop' hangman. Before Marwood's time the process of hanging was, in most cases, a form of slow strangulation and his method was regarded as more humane. By his 'long-drop' method he claimed the victim's neck was broken by the sudden jerk on the rope.

Marwood was chosen from a large number of applicants, all eager to occupy the post of public hangman. The candidates coming from all ranks of society, among them butchers, sailors, soldiers, clerks and doctors. Although the applicants hailed from all parts of the country, the greatest number were from Lancashire.

The new hangman followed the trade of cobbler and he lived all his life at Horncastle in Lincolnshire, where he was born in 1820.

Over the door of his little cobbler's shop in Horncastle, he had printed in large letters: 'MARWOOD, CROWN OFFICE'

The shop was a small, one-storeyed place, close to the church.

William Marwood – within a year of his appointment as executioner, he was called to Lancaster to despatch Preston killer Mark Fiddler

He was, in fact, very proud of his new position, although when it first became knowledge in Horncastle, he was, for some months, hooted and hissed at whenever he appeared in the streets. Marwood developed a very high view of his office and was happy to say, "I am doing God's work, according to the Divine Command and the law of the British Crown. I do it simply as a matter of duty and as a Christian. I sleep as soundly as a child and am never disturbed by phantoms. Where there is guilt there is bad sleeping, but I am conscious that I live a blameless life. Detesting idleness, I pass my vacant time in business. It would have been better for those I executed if they had preferred industry to idleness."

The prison authorities at Lancaster Castle enlisting his services in August, 1875 for the double execution of William McCullough from Barrow and Mark Fiddler from Preston. There was a great deal of local sympathy for Fiddler, who had killed his wife and an openly published letter and verse to his mother-in-law added to the feelings of sadness.

Marwood though, hanged the pair with his usual efficiency taking care not to become involved in any sentimentality He was in fact a very mild man, who could always be seen kneeling down and praying to God for the man whose life he was about to take.

A man of middle height with broad, compactly-set shoulders, he dressed for the executions in such a coat as a Lincolnshire farmer would wear, with high

A few more suns shall set
O'er these dark hills of time,
And we shall be where suns are not,
A far serener clime.

Then, O! my Lord, prepare
My soul for that bless'd day;
O wash me in Thy precious blood,
And take my sins away.

A few more struggles here,
A few more partings o'er,
A few more toils, a few more tears,
And we shall weep no more.

Then, O my Lord, prepare
My soul for that bright day;
O wash me in Thy precious blood,
And take my sins away.

Amen!—Good Night.

black stockings and low felt hat.

Like his predecessors, Marwood received threats against his life. He was asked on one occasion if he was nervous of the work he had to do and he replied, "England does not send nervous men out on a job of this kind."

Besides his expenses, Marwood received £10 for each execution and the City of London paid him an annual retaining fee of £20.

His death occurred at the beginning of September, 1883 the cause being inflammation of the lungs, aggravated by jaundice.

A letter and a verse written from his condemned cell earned sympathy for Mark Fiddler of Preston

Lancaster Castle, 11th August, 1875.

Dear Mother-in-law,—I write these few lines to you, hoping to find you all well, as it leaves me at present, thank God for it. Dear Mother, I hope you will let your Sisters know, and your sons William and John and James, and your dear Husband, that you have received this letter from me. And I hope that you will forgive me for my past conduct, and I feel that I ought to say, that anything in Dorothy's conduct that was not perfect would have been so if I had been a good husband; for I am quite sure that she would have done her part if I had done mine. But I hope this my case will be a warning to all men not to take heed of anything said about their wives; for you see what a disgrace I am to my relations and friends, and I feel very sorry indeed when I think of my youth, how foolish I have been; but I have prayed to God to forgive me, and He has, I am sure. I pray for you all, and I pray for my dear Wife Dorothy, if I can do her any good. But I hope God will hear my prayer, for she had no time to repent. But God is good; He can forgive to the last moment, and I hope He has forgiven her. So no more at present from your son-in-law,
MARK FIDDLER.

THE END